101 Questions and Answers on Confucianism, Daoism, and Shinto

101 QUESTIONS AND ANSWERS ON CONFUCIANISM, DAOISM, AND SHINTO

John Renard

PAULIST PRESS
New York/Mahwah, N.J.

Library of Congress Cataloging-in-Publication Data

Renard, John, 1944–
   101 Questions and answers on Confucianism, Daoism, and Shinto / John Renard.
     p. cm.
   Includes bibliographical references.
   ISBN 0-8091-4091-8
   1. Confucianism—Miscellanea. 2. Taoism—Miscellanea. 3. Shinto—Miscellanea. I. Title: One hundred one questions and answers on Confucianism, Daoism, and Shinto. II. Title.
BL1853 .R4 2002
299'.5—dc21

                                       2002007620

Published by Paulist Press
997 Macarthur Boulevard
Mahwah, New Jersey 07430

www.paulistpress.com

Printed and bound in the
United States of America

CONTENTS

v

PREFACE

Confucianism, Daoism, and Shinto. Reference to the three great "-isms" that typically head up the list of ancient indigenous traditions of China and Japan often raises the questions "Are they authentically religious? Are they not rather ethical or philosophical traditions?" Some scholars argue that the teachings customarily identified as "Confucianism" constitute a system of ethics or political philosophy rather than a system of religious beliefs. Imperial ritual, on the other hand, might qualify as an authentically religious phenomenon because it pays homage to deities called Heaven and Earth. Neither, however, has a distinct "ecclesiastical" structure, officially ordained priesthood, or scriptures that claim the authority of divine revelation. Nevertheless, Confucian tradition has many important features that might identify it as a religious tradition, partly because it has been historically so intertwined with the Chinese imperial cult and partly because of its strong sense of the sacred in ordinary human experience. Those features include an acknowledgment of transcendent power called the Dao, manifest in Heaven and Earth, and the long-standing reverence of Confucius as a Holy One on a par with Heaven and Earth.

Religious studies scholars more and more have come to appreciate the genuinely religious qualities of Shinto. Every now and then criticism still surfaces that Shinto is so much a part of ordinary Japanese life that it is really a set of cultural beliefs and practices rather than a religious tradition. Some critics base their conclusion on polls of the Japanese public that seem to suggest widespread apathy about religious issues. Decreasing numbers of people are willing to identify themselves as adherents of any religious tradition, including Shinto. Others focus on the phenomenon that even Japanese who do consider themselves active participants in a Shinto-based community are likely to claim that they are Buddhist as well. Doesn't that suggest that Shinto is less than authentically religious? If it were, some argue, it would hardly tolerate multiple religious allegiances, would it? Some point to Shinto's apparently total concern with the ordinary, the everyday, the natural world that surrounds us, and lack of interest in transcendent mystery. Surely a religious tradition ought to be more invested in turning people's attention to a world beyond this one? In fact, these and other distinctive aspects of Shinto are among its strengths and unique contributions to our world. Shinto offers arresting insights into the inherently divine quality of the simplest things, the beauty hidden away in life's nooks and crannies. Beneath the appearances of things, Shinto tradition discerns innumerable causes for profound gratitude to the powers beyond the merely human that make life itself possible. Shinto may not be celebrated for producing sophisticated schools of theological speculation, but it undoubtedly possesses many characteristics that identify it as a religious tradition.

While it is certainly true that ethical and/or philosophical dimensions are prominent in all three traditions, so are features generally identified as religious and sacred. They include, for example, sacred texts, rituals directed to powers or beings that transcend ordinary human experience, sacred spaces dedicated to the practice of those rituals, community structures focused on the practice and furtherance of those rituals and their underlying beliefs, and a differentiation among adherents as to specialists and non-specialists. For these and a host of other reasons that will become apparent as the reader progresses through the book, I have concluded that one can justifiably call the Confucian, Daoist, and Shinto traditions religious.

In addition, I have maintained two further distinctions with respect to the Chinese religious traditions. Religious Daoism and Confucianism in its "religious" dimensions have long been associated with other prominent currents in Chinese religious history, but they are not identical with them. Scholars have devised labels such as "Chinese Popular Religion" (or even Popular Daoism) to distinguish a broader strain of belief and practice that, while it intersects or overlaps at points with both Daoism proper and Buddhism, nevertheless suggests enough distinctive features to warrant a category of its own. Here I have opted for the term "Chinese Community Traditions" (or CCT) to refer to that dimension of Chinese religious life. Confucian tradition, similarly, has historically been intertwined with the life and fortunes of the Chinese imperial court. But the court had its rituals and specialists that were distinctive, even as they intersected or overlapped at some points with Confucian tradition. I have opted for the term "Chinese Imperial Tradition" (CIT for short) in reference to the "religious" aspects of court life and administration.

This volume is the fourth in a matched set of short introductions to major religious traditions to be produced in Paulist Press's "101 Questions" series. To provide ready cross-referencing, I have structured the material in nine sections very similar to those of the earlier volumes on Islam, Hinduism, and Buddhism. Since this volume surveys more than one tradition, some questions in each section dealing with larger topics provide information on one tradition alone, while others treat lesser themes by setting a look at all three traditions side by side within one response. Section one offers an overview of origins and sacred texts, with section two expanding somewhat on later developments both historical and theological. Section three, on doctrines and practices, deals with large theological concepts, such as revelation, salvation, views of human life both here and hereafter, as well as the main outlines of ritual life. Section four surveys the larger elements of ethical and legal concerns, along with hierarchical and other structures of religious authority. In section five, central themes of spirituality and popular piety include the categories of mystic, miracle, relic, and saint, for example, and various aspects of popular devotional life. Selected themes relating to the visual and other modes (e.g., performance arts such as music and dance) of artistic expression of religious values occupy section six, while a summary of major issues in the three traditions' internal diversity and relations with other traditions come to the fore in section seven. Section eight covers a range of matters concerning women, the family, and social/community processes. A look at a variety of topics focused on the shape of these major traditions in our time concludes the questions.

I am hugely indebted to scores of scholars dedicated to Chinese and Japanese religious studies for the information contained in these pages. Any misinterpretation or misconstrual of data their works have provided is solely my responsibility. Two things have occasioned this book: opportunities to travel over the past twenty years in China, Taiwan, Japan, and Korea, as well as elsewhere in the East, Southeast Asia, and the Pacific where adherents of these great traditions live and practice; and thirty years of teaching courses on religious and artistic traditions of Asia at both the secondary and university levels. I am particularly grateful to Martin Connors, publisher of Visible Ink Press, for permission to publish here a heavily revised version of the final three chapters of a larger survey of major religious traditions. Special thanks to Ryan Harshman for providing the index. Many thanks to Kathleen Walsh of Paulist Press, for her willingness to add this material to the "101 Questions" series, to Chris Bellitto for seeing it to completion, and to Father Kevin Lynch of Paulist for initiating the whole process nearly five years ago with an invitation to do the Islam volume. And, as always, my deepest gratitude to my wife, Mary Pat, for her unfailing support and good humor.

ONE:

BEGINNINGS AND EARLY SOURCES

1. Who was *Confucius* and what do traditional accounts tell us about his life?

Confucius was born around 551 B.C.E. and died in 479 B.C.E., an almost exact contemporary of the Buddha. The name by which he is most commonly known, Confucius, is a Latinized form of Kongfuzi, Venerable Master Kong. According to tradition, his mother, Yan Zheng Zai, had prayed on Mount Ni that she would have a child. Confucius's father, Shu Liang He, died when the child was three years old, and his mother raised him under difficult circumstances. At nineteen, Confucius married and had a son and a daughter. His not very happy marriage would end with the death of his wife, and his son died during Confucius's life. At twenty-two, he began the first of several jobs for the state of Lu. At twenty-six (some say thirty-three), Confucius went to the Zhou dynasty's imperial capital of Lu to study royal ceremony and seek a government position. There he is said to have met the aged Laozi. Traditional accounts of that meeting (with a decidedly Daoist slant) report that Laozi took Confucius to task for wasting effort on formal study and reliance on ethical absolutes. He would do far better to observe how nature accomplishes all good things without contrivance, effortlessly. Still Confucius pursued his laborious path.

He spent many years teaching privately and sought to win converts to his ethical and political views. At about fifty, he took a minor governmental post. But he failed to gain the public recognition he craved. Hoping to find a willing political patron, he went into a thirteen-year self-imposed exile, wandering in and out of nine provinces. Confucius returned home at the age of sixty-eight, there to spend his last five years studying and editing the Classics. The Master had a passion for fostering the kind of order in society that he felt sure could offer genuine happiness. He sought to articulate a view of the individual who could contribute to society through self-mastery and personal responsibility.

2. What are the *origins of "Confucianism"*? Who were the *Literati*?

"Confucianism" refers to the system of social, ethical, and religious beliefs and practices associated with Confucius. The term does not imply the worship of Confucius as a supreme or central deity, but it does acknowledge his foundational and pivotal role in the cultivation of beliefs and practices that have remained important in many Asian societies for centuries. Some scholars suggest that we replace "Confucianism" with "Literati Tradition" to indicate that the complex of beliefs and practices now generally attributed to Confucius is actually part of a broader cultural phenomenon. "Literati" (the Latin for "the lettered, educated") is a name coined by non-Chinese scholars to describe a cultural elite most influential in promoting and preserving the Chinese imperial system. The Literati were the highly educated, professionally specialized bureaucrats who maintained the far-flung governmental structures of the empire. They also functioned as the ritual specialists in the many religious ceremonies performed under imperial sponsorship. Confucius was one of these Literati, but he and the movement that bears his name have also had a life of their own. The Literati were the social class most responsible for maintaining all the mechanisms of the imperial administration. One of their chief tools was an elaborate system of training that culminated in "civil service" examinations (the grandfather of all civil service systems) and the awarding of degrees. When the imperial examination system was abolished in 1905 in favor of more modern educational methods, the Literati began to disappear as a social class. In 1911, the last emperor was deposed, ending three millennia of Chinese imperial rule. But Confucius did not die with the Literati and the empire. Over the centuries he had become an important part of Chinese culture. He was both a symbol of the best in Chinese tradition and a man revered religiously as well. There is some overlapping, therefore, among these three developments—Confucianism, the Literati Tradition, and the Chinese Imperial Tradition (CIT)—but they are not identical. Think of them as a railway that has sometimes run along a single track and sometimes branched off into two or three parallel tracks along the same broad right-of-way. In short, all Literati were Confucians, and since the CIT in general incorporated Confucian philosophy, the Literati became the official "staff" of the CIT. But not all those who considered themselves Confucians were Literati. And with the end of the empire came the end of the Literati as a cultural/religious elite.

3. How is the *Chinese Imperial Tradition* (CIT) related to "Confucianism"?

Long before the time of Confucius, a system of beliefs and practices had developed around the role of the emperor in cosmic affairs. The Chinese had come to regard the emperor as the Son of Heaven. He bore the awesome responsibility of securing the welfare of all his subjects by discerning and executing faithfully the Will (or Mandate) of Heaven. Though the emperor was called Son of Heaven, he was not considered a deity. He was, rather, one who had the ultimate sanction for exercising authority on earth, so long as he maintained contact with the heavenly mandate. Whenever a ruler failed to see that his people enjoyed universal justice, the people could justifiably conclude that Heaven's mandate had passed to a more worthy leader. Revolution was the solution. The CIT had its pantheon of deities arranged in several hierarchical levels, so that the earthly royal administration appeared to mirror the heavenly. The CIT did not revolve around a sacred scripture, nor did it have a separate "ecclesiastical" structure or ordained priesthood. It did, however, have its own equivalent of religious doctrine, elaborate rituals comparable in form and content to those of many major religious traditions, and a hierarchical organization complete with ritual specialists. The

CIT is an integral part of the religious history of China, since it formed the broad backdrop against which nearly the whole of that history has been played out.

The CIT's formal recognition of members of its pantheon went through many changes over the course of more than three thousand years. Here are some of the principal features of this vast and rather fluid phenomenon. Deities and heavenly powers generally fit into a three-level system. At the top were the powers deemed most necessary to cosmic survival. Ancient tradition includes belief in a mysterious celestial power called Shangdi. Eventually the word *di* came to be the standard term now translated as "emperor." But Shangdi was still the "supreme emperor." Standard Chinese religious usage also referred to *Tian,* Heaven, as a generic term for the region in which Shangdi lived. Neither Shangdi nor Tian was a personal deity actively involved in human affairs, but represented a more impersonal source of all things manifest in the universe. Also on the top level were the royal ancestors, the spirits of earth and grain, and the Earth, sometimes referred to as "empress" to Heaven's "emperor."

But there was yet another power behind Shangdi and Tian. That was the Dao, whose eternal energies of Yang (male principle, dry, bright, and evident) and Yin (female principle, moist, dark, and mysterious) are manifest in the universe and made known to humanity as the Will of Heaven. At the invisible "juncture" of Yin and Yang is the transcendent form of pure natural energy known as *qi,* found in its fullness wherever Yin and Yang are in perfect balance.

A notch lower came the principal heavenly bodies, Sun and Moon, and Jupiter, whose revolutions of the sun determine the ritual calendar. Rulers of earlier dynasties, patrons of farming and silk cultivation, and the spirits of Heaven and Earth round out the second level. Confucius was once a member of the second rank, but was elevated by imperial decree to the first in 1907.

At the third level the CIT begins to overlap somewhat with Daoism and Chinese Community Traditions (CCT), with their more specialized and local deities. Here are gathered the deities of fire, literature, war, artillery, soil, mechanical arts, the hearth, the granary, and the home threshold. Along with the patron deity of Beijing are three dragon deities associated with the city. Finally, several historical heroes fit here as well. A deity called Guandi or Guangong deserves special mention as a cross-over figure important in more than one pantheon. Guandi is known by a wide variety of names, depending on the constituency of worshipers. Many people identify him as the God of War, though the red-faced, full-bearded deity is chiefly a paragon of civic virtue. The emperor had the authority to rearrange, shrink, or expand the pantheon. He could simply decree a spirit worthy of a particular rank and eventually even declare worship of that being the practice of the realm by instituting temples in his or her honor.

4. What were the earliest *Confucian sacred texts*? Has Confucian tradition included any other sacred texts in its canon?

A set of works called the *Five Classics (Wujing)* became a formal collection sometime during the Han dynasty (206 B.C.E.–220 C.E.). The *Yijing,* or *Classic of Change,* is a manual of divination dating from the early Zhou dynasty (c. 1040–256 B.C.E.). The *Yijing* assists practitioners in the interpretation of fundamental life choices by "reading" a set of divining sticks for the pattern they reveal when thrown down. Although it was originally designed as a descriptive device, popular usage over the centuries has bestowed on the book powers of prognostication. The *Classic of History (Shujing)* assembles historical documents from as early as 600 B.C.E. to as late as 200 C.E.

An anthology of over three hundred poems, some from as early as 800 to 600 B.C.E., is called the *Classic of Poetry (Shijing).* Ancient tradition that Confucius himself had compiled the material from a larger collection of over three thousand pieces is probably inaccurate. But it does appear that Confucius and his disciples used the poems as sources of ethical example. Completed around

100 C.E. of material from much earlier times, the *Classic of Rites (Liji)* preserves ceremonial records that offer essential insights into ritual life. It eventually became one of three texts on "rites" known collectively (with the *Ceremonial and Ritual* or *Yi Li* and the *Officials of the Zhou [dynasty]* or *Zhouli)* as the *Lijing.* Finally, the *Annals of Spring and Autumn (Chunqiu)* chronicles events in Confucius's home province of Lu from 722 to 481 B.C.E. (called the period of Spring and Autumn), and the tradition that Confucius edited the text seems to be accurate.

A second collection called the *Four Books (Ssu Shu)* consists of very ancient texts eventually brought together during the Song dynasty (960–1279 C.E.). Most famous of the four is a work commonly called the *Analects (Lun Yu),* a compilation of Confucius's sayings and dialogues edited by second-generation disciples around 400 B.C.E. *The Great Learning (Daxue)* is a chapter excerpted from the *Classic of Rites,* singled out now as a separate book because of its centrality to Confucian thought. Dating to about 350 B.C.E., this work is probably the single most important statement of Confucian views on the cultivation of the ideal human being, or "superior person," essential to a harmonious society. Another excerpt from the *Classic of Rites* is now regarded as a separate book called the *Doctrine of the Mean (Zhong Yong),* traditionally attributed to Confucius's grandson Zu Ssu. Its theme is the harmonious development of human nature by means of right action and the principle of reciprocity as manifest in the five fundamental relationships. Finally, the *Mengzi* includes the largely ethical and political teachings of Mengzi (c. 372–289 B.C.E.), commonly known as Mencius. He was one of the foundational figures in the interpretation of the classic Literati themes expounded by Confucius. The book's seven sections emphasize the need for vigilance in cultivating virtue with the ultimate goal of living in harmony with the Will (or Mandate) of Heaven. By about 1200 C.E., the complete Literati "canon" of texts included not only the *Five Classics* and the *Four Books,* but four other works considered to contain the essentials of Confucian and Literati views on all things under Heaven.

5. Who was *Laozi*, and what was his connection with the origins of religious Daoism and its scriptures?

Laozi was likely an altogether legendary figure whose name simply means "old teacher or master." Tradition says he was born around 604 B.C.E., making him a much older contemporary of Confucius (Kongzi, 551–479 B.C.E.), who was in turn an almost exact contemporary of the Buddha. The legend says Laozi was a clerk in the archives of the Zhou dynasty who practiced the "Way and its power" and emphasized self-effacement and anonymity. When he became convinced that social disintegration and political corruption in the Zhou dynasty were irreversible, he decided to withdraw from society. Riding his water buffalo, the old man came to the frontier. There a customs officer begged him to write down his lofty teachings before departing. Laozi wrote the *Daodejing* (the *Classic of the Way and Its Power*) and disappeared, leaving a legacy of mystery.

Though tradition attributes it to Laozi, the *Daodejing* actually dates from between 300 and 250 B.C.E. and remains the signature text of Daoism. Its authorship and immediate historical context remain uncertain. Its attribution to the "Old Master" may have arisen out of a desire to lend the text greater legitimacy and credibility. The *Daodejing*'s eighty-one tantalizing short poems brim with paradox as they try to describe the indescribable by saying what it is *not*. Just as the value of a cup is the emptiness within, for example, so the Way progresses by (apparently) going backward. As all of nature acts without conscious effort, so the person who strives in hope of gain loses all. The curiously attractive teaching of the *Daodejing* emphasizes the Way of utter simplicity. The text is divided into two parts: poems one to thirty-seven focus on the Way, poems thirty-eight to eighty-one on its Power. Some describe the Way as the passive principle and its Power as primal spiritual energy. Anyone who tries to define the Way must know that it remains indefinable. Dao is the source of all energy but eludes discovery. Imperceptible yet irresistible, impersonal yet ever-present, the Dao's power is like that of the action of water on stone or iron: the softest of all elements inevitably dissolves the hardest.

Much later stories, perhaps from a time when Daoists and Confucians were in competition for followers, tell of a meeting between Laozi and a youthful Confucius. No use wasting so much time studying your history, Laozi counseled the newcomer. Observe nature and you will see that love for the Dao is all that one needs. Popular tradition tends to identify Laozi as the one who first taught that ordinary folk could seek and attain immortality. Some scholars suggest that Laozi's stature may have been enhanced as a result of his mistaken identification with the legendary Huangdi, known as the Yellow Emperor, who ruled in the mid-third millennium B.C.E. Laozi was officially declared a god around 666 C.E. and eventually became part of a much-expanded Daoist pantheon.

6. What is *religious Daoism* and how does it differ from *"Chinese Community Traditions"* (CCT)?

"Daoism" refers to a wide range of philosophical, religious, and magical traditions dating from perhaps the fourth century B.C.E. in China. Here the focus will be on the specifically religious aspects of these complex and ancient traditions. The most ancient roots of Daoism are in shamanistic cults dating back perhaps several millennia to prehistoric China. Celebrated imperial figures of that age, Yu, Shun, and Yao, are still revered as great sages. According to legend, Daoism formally began with Laozi's writing of the *Daodejing,* the *Classic of the Way and Its Power* in the sixth century B.C.E. Scholars now believe the *Daodejing* actually dates from between 300 and 250 B.C.E. Teachings of the *Daodejing* came together with those of thinkers like Yang Zhu (340–266 B.C.E.) and Zhuang Zi (369–286 B.C.E.) to form the broad conceptual basis of a wider "Daoist" tradition that had become largely philosophical *(Daojia)* by the fourth century B.C.E. But religious Daoism *(Daojiao)* was still a long way off. Solid scholarly research suggests that Daoism as a religious tradition begins in the mid-second century C.E. It seems a teacher named Zhang Daoling (34–156 C.E.) claimed that Laozi himself commissioned him to spread the teaching of the Dao. Zhang inaugurated the Five Bushels of Rice movement (a reference to the suggested offering for would-be members) and built a religious polity in Szechuan province. According to legend, Zhang Daoling's emphasis on acquiring immortality culminated in his ascension into the heavens. Out of that movement grew the first and one of the most influential branches of religious Daoism, the Celestial Masters school. Religious Daoism has since developed numerous sects and schools, each with its distinctive emphasis on various spiritual teachings and ritual practices.

Much more ancient than religious or even earlier philosophical Daoism are the various currents of popular religious belief and practice that together comprise what I will refer to as Chinese Community Traditions or CCT. Historians of religion suggest that most Chinese who engage in public expression of religious beliefs actually belong to this broad popular stream. Many of their beliefs have Daoist connections, but, unlike Daoism as such, CCT has not been associated with formal religious institutions such as priesthood and monastic orders, and does not possess a scriptural canon. Many beliefs and practices now widespread in popular tradition also have roots in ancient Confucian and imperial cultic institutions, and in Buddhism as well. Countless CCT temples began to appear in towns and villages several centuries ago. Since they do not have their own resident ritual specialists, these temples often enlist the services of Daoist priests, but day-to-day services are often handled by dedicated lay persons. Many such temples are associated with families, who maintain them as a public service and as family tradition.

Some elements of CCT also appear in temples ostensibly identified as Buddhist. A Guanyin temple in Honolulu, for example, combines Buddhist rituals with a host of other popular practices. Though the main image is that of the Buddha, numerous other icons are prominently displayed. That particular temple is run by a group of Chinese Buddhist nuns who are especially concerned with preserving the image that theirs is a purely Buddhist temple, in spite of the obvious diversity within it. When I asked permission to snap a few photos inside, the nun in charge said yes. But whenever she thought my camera lens was wandering toward Confucius or another icon, she tugged my sleeve and waved a disapproving finger at me. "Only Buddha," she insisted. Just a few blocks away, above a small upholstery shop, is the Lum family temple. There all the deities are clearly of the CCT variety, even though some are often inaccurately identified as Daoist.

7. Were there other important *Daoist scriptures?* And did an official *canon of Daoist sacred texts* ever develop?

A text known as the *Zhuangzi,* after the man whose disciples may have authored it, dates from about the fourth century B.C.E. The work is also known as the *Divine Classic of Nan Hua,* the town to which Zhuangzi was believed to have retired. Zhuangzi the Daoist philosopher (c. 389–286 B.C.E.) remains a relatively little known figure. But the work that bears his name stands out as a foundational document in philosophical Daoism. The document's interpretation of basic concepts also influenced many religious Daoists. In addition to its bold attacks on the inadequacy of Confucian teaching, the *Zhuangzi* presents essentially the same worldview as the *Daodejing,* especially the importance of non-effort *(wu wei)* or "unmotivated action" and its political implications. The *Zhuangzi* emphasizes the concepts of longevity and immortality that would later take on great significance for many religious Daoists. Perhaps more important is the concept of mental purification called "fasting of the heart (or mind)," a practice in which the individual meditates on nature to achieve a simplified awareness. Zhuangzi's teaching, which speaks often of an experience of oneness with the Dao, has become an important element in Daoist mysticism.

A Daoist philosopher named Liezi is likewise said to have penned a work that bears his name. That book, also known as *The True Classic of Expanding Emptiness,* however, was almost certainly of a later time, and Liezi is probably a legendary figure. Containing materials of many different literary types, especially narrative forms such as anecdotes and parables, the book was probably compiled around 300 C.E. Its eight chapters arrange their literarily disparate materials thematically, addressing such topics as fate and human freedom, problems in establishing ethical standards, and the challenge of following the Dao.

Around 471 Lu Xiujing (406–77 C.E.) compiled the earliest formal attempt at a Daoist canon. His work only catalogued important works, but there would eventually be seven major edited collections of Daoist sacred texts. Between about 1000 and 1250 C.E., five enormous collections would appear. The final product was a large anthology of separate texts organized in three sections and published in its present form in 1444 C.E. The triple division of the canonical collection, called the *Daozang,* may have been associated with, or perhaps a response to, the Buddhist scriptural canon known as the "Three Baskets." Each is named after one of the three heavens that were the abodes of the Three Pure Ones and begins with a major text said to have been revealed by one of the Pure Ones. The *Daozang*'s three parts include 1,476 disparate works in over five thousand scroll-volumes. Every imaginable variety of text is available in the modern sixty-volume reprint of the canon. Twelve sub-divisions arrange the material this way: primal revelations, talismans, scriptural interpretation (or exegesis), sacred diagrams, historical texts, ethical texts, ritual texts, practical techniques, biographical information, sacred songs, and memorials. Most of the various sects and schools of Daoism focus on one or a select few of the many possibilities the canon offers. As we shall see later, recitation or chanting of sacred texts forms an important part of some ritual observances.

8. What is *Shinto* and what are its *origins?*

"Shinto" derives from two Chinese words, *shen* meaning "deity" and *dao* meaning "way." The Japanese reading of the Chinese expression comes out *Kami no Michi,* the "Path of the *Kami.*" Since at least several centuries B.C.E., the Japanese had acknowledged the sacred presence and power of numinous beings called *kami,* "high or superior ones." Until about the middle of the sixth century C.E., the Japanese people evidently did not think of their ancient religious traditions as a separate system. So organically integrated were those traditions with their entire culture and heritage that worship of the *kami* was largely assumed as *the* Japanese way. Only with the arrival of Buddhism, called in Japanese the "Way of the Buddha" *(Butsu-do),* did it become necessary to give the indigenous beliefs and practices a name to distinguish them from this imported tradition. Unlike many other major traditions, Shinto had neither a founder nor a single foundational figure who represents concrete historical origins. In a sense, Shinto is as old as Japan itself, somewhat the way Hinduism is as old as India. At its core, the Way of the *Kami* enshrines profound insights into the sacred character of all created nature. Shinto calls people to a deep awareness of the divine presence suffusing all things, to the challenge of personal and corporate responsibility for the stewardship of the world that is home, to unending gratitude for all that is good, and to a willingness to seek purification and forgiveness for humanly inevitable lapses. Observe worshipers at a Shinto shrine—as Buddhism has temples, Shinto has shrines—and there can be little doubt of the sincere devotion that moves so many people to prayer and ritual expression of their beliefs.

9. What are the earliest important *Shinto sacred texts?*

Two eighth-century documents are Shinto's foundational texts. These are among the youngest of the major religious traditions' primary works. Unlike many other sacred texts, they are not considered to have been divinely written, even though their subject matter is of divine origin. In other words, these scriptures are not considered divine communication as such, but communication about things divine. The *Records of Ancient Matters,* or *Kojiki,* dates to 712 C.E. Composed by a courtier named Yasumaro, its three volumes deal with events beginning with the creation of the Japanese islands and people and continuing down to 628 C.E. Exegetes have authored scores of major commentaries (called *kojikiden*) in relatively recent times. The thirty-volume *Chronicles of Japan,* called *Nihongi* as well as *Nihon Shoki,* was completed in 720 C.E. About three times the length of the *Kojiki,* the *Chronicles of Japan* also recount the ancient cosmogonic myth, though in a less detailed fashion. Greater detail about subsequent imperial history includes events up to 697 C.E. These two texts enjoyed special prominence after the seventeenth century, when a school of Shinto studies called "National Learning" (Kokugaku) set out to probe the sources for the essence of Japanese-ness that they communicate. These primary texts are so important because they record the history of the imperial family and legitimate its authority by establishing its divine lineage.

10. Were Shinto's sacred texts ever gathered into a *formal scriptural canon?*

Scholars refer to the various sacred texts collectively as *shinten,* "texts of the deities." But even though they generally agree on the importance of a certain set of works, there has never been an official process of "canonization" by which representatives of the tradition have formally declared certain texts as definitive. Here are the most important of the classical documents, beyond the *Kojiki* and *Nihongi.* From the early eighth century, the *Records of Wind and Earth (Fudoki)* provides data about very early religious rituals from major shrines. The early ninth-century *Kogo-shui* (807 C.E.), or *Gleaning of Ancient Words,* comments on previous documents in an attempt to legitimate the Imbe family against their enemies, the Nakatomi clan.

The *Manyoshu,* or *Collection of Countless Leaves,* anthologizes a large selection of seventh- and eighth-century Japanese poetry of various genres. Some Shinto scholars have insisted that these poems represent the purest form of Japanese literary expression. First published in 927, the *Engi-shiki* includes a collection of over two dozen prayer texts. A work called the *Kujiki* (also *Sendai Kuji Hongi*) or *Records of Ancient Happenings,* bears the date 620 but was probably composed as late as the ninth century to compete with the similar sounding *Kojiki* in antiquity and authority. It amounts to what some traditions might call an "apocryphal" work—not what it claims to be, but still full of valuable material. Finally, a group of thirteenth-century texts called the *Five Shinto Scriptures (Shinto gobusho)* emphasize the antiquity of Japan's Shinto heritage.

11. Are there important *"mythic" elements* in these traditions?

Confucianism/CIT: Confucius looked to history for lessons about life. The stories he found to have the greatest educational value were those about human beings, the truly great and the mean-spirited alike, who had shaped life in the Middle Kingdom for good or ill. The high exemplars were themselves people, the rulers and sages of old. Like his Indian contemporary the Buddha, Confucius preferred not to commit his time and energy to discrediting the stories of the gods and super-human heroes of his culture. He was simply convinced that, whatever their powers and prerogatives, the subjects of China's myths could not relieve human beings of their most fundamental responsibilities. The ultimate divine favor, Confucius believed, was a climate in which people could turn their full attention to the everyday realities of family, livelihood, and the betterment of society. Still, under pressure from Daoism and Buddhism, later Confucians cloaked the birth and life of the Master in wondrous tales. A unicorn presaged Confucius's birth by presenting his mother with a tablet of announcement, a pair of dragons and five ancient men symbolizing the five directions appeared in the heavens on the day he was born, and a celestial musical ensemble provided accompaniment for his birth. The CIT likewise did not revolve around mythic narratives as such. Divinely sanctioned representatives of the people under Heaven had more pressing concerns. But the emperor had the power to elevate individual heroes and gods from local to universal stature. As a result he was, ironically perhaps, China's most important myth-maker.

Daoism: Daoist stories of how the world came to be are full of mythic features similar to those of other cosmogonies. They talk of how order overcame chaos, how the heavens and earth came to be separated, and how the innumerable deities—thirty-six thousand according to one reckoning—fit into the grand picture. What is unique and most interesting about Daoist myth is that the gods do not necessarily take an active role in cosmic affairs. They do not intervene in the unfolding cosmos, nor even nudge the process along for that matter. Instead they allow the fundamental laws of creation itself to operate unimpeded. Indeed, the gods themselves come into being as part of this whole unfolding set in motion by an impersonal power called Heaven. What good are the deities then? They, along with the spiritually accomplished ones called sages and immortals, instruct humankind in the ways to achieve salvation. A clue to the place of many of these celestial beings in the grand scheme of things is their connection with the stars. Dozens of the members of the Daoist and popular Chinese pantheons are or have been associated with specific heavenly bodies or constellations. They are thus both visible and impossibly distant.

Shinto: Two of the earliest of Shinto's foundational documents recount the story of the divine origins of Japan and its people. In variant accounts, the *Kojiki* and *Nihongi* tell of how Japan came into existence, but the myth is not so much a narrative of creation as it is of Japan's unique sacred history. The basic myth goes like this: In the beginning, Heaven and Earth were as one, like positive and negative unseparated. In a primal egg-like mass dwelt the principles of all life. Eventually the purer, lighter element rose and became heaven, while the heavier descended to form earth. A reed-shoot grew between earth and heaven and became the "One who established the Eternal Land." After some aeons, two *kami* formed by spontaneous generation. Descending to earth on the Floating Bridge of Heaven, Izanagi, the Male Who Invites, and Izanami, the Female Who Invites, came into the world. In an image of sexual procreation, Izanagi stirred the ocean depths with his spear and created the first lands.

On the eight Japanese islands the union of the Male and Female produced the mountains and rivers, and thirty-five other *kami*. Last to be born was Fire, the *kami* of heat, who burned his mother fatally during his birth. Izanagi slew Fire with his sword, creating numerous additional *kami* in the process. The Female fled to the underworld, the Land of Darkness, desperate to prevent her husband from seeing her corrupted state. When the Male followed and lit a fire so that he could see, she chased him out and blocked the entry to the underworld. Returning to the surface, the Male immediately purified himself ritually, ridding himself of the underworld's pollution. Corruption from his left eye formed the sun goddess, Amaterasu who rules the High Plain of Heaven, and from his right, Tsukiyomi, the moon, whose province is the oceans. From his nostrils he created the storm *kami*, Susanowo, Withering Wind of Summer and ruler of the earth. Susanowo soon made trouble for his sister, the Sun, who took refuge in a rock cave. Needing the sun to return, the eight hundred thousand *kami* conferred as to how they might entice her from her cave. At length they resorted to enlisting the Terrible Female of Heaven to dance and shout obscenities to rouse Amaterasu's curiosity. They then offered her blue and white soft offerings, a mirror, and a bejeweled Sakaki tree. She finally came out and dispatched her grandson Ninigi to rule the world. His son in turn, Jimmu Tenno, became the first human emperor at age forty-five, on February 11, 660 B.C.E.

12. Who are some of the *principal Shinto deities,* apart from those mentioned in the primal myth?

Hachiman, generally identified as the *kami* of war, is near the top of the pantheon. It is no surprise that he often appears in painting and sculpture as armed and dangerous. But some of the most famous images portray Hachiman as a meditating monk or solicitous bodhisattva, reflecting Buddhism's influence. Almost fifty thousand shrines honor Hachiman.

A curious grouping called the "Seven Gods of Good Luck" *(shichi-fuku-jin)* brings together figures of mixed background. Daikoku (sometimes called Daikoku-ten) hails from India, mythologically speaking, and probably traveled to Japan with an early influential Buddhist founder named Saicho. Daikoku is associated with accomplishment of one's goals and with wealth. Stone statues show a jovial bruiser with a sack over one shoulder, sitting on bales of rice and wielding a mallet with which he grants wishes. Also a god of prosperity, Ebisu is especially popular in fishing villages, rice farms, and local marketplaces. Ebisu is deaf and fails to hear deities being called together for his own October celebration! Like Daikoku, Bishamon (also Bishamonten) is of Indian origin. In the Hindu pantheon he was one of the four heavenly guardians, presiding over the north. In Buddhist as well as Shinto iconography, Bishamon is heavily armed and holds a miniature pagoda in his left hand as a symbol of his authority. Fuku-roku-ju, who originated in Daoism, stands for happiness, fortune, and long life, as his name indicates. When depicted in the arts he looks very much like his Chinese counterpart, Shou Lao, generally accompanied by a crane or deer. Like the next God of Good Luck, Jurojin, he also has a walking stick to which he has attached a sacred text. Jurojin is another patron of longevity of Daoist origin. Hotei, likewise drawn from the Daoist pantheon, stands for happiness and wealth. Benzaiten, also known as Benten, is the lone female of the bunch. The septet of good fortune *kami* have been a favorite subject for popular and charming miniature carvings called *netsuke.* A large number of *kami* are associated with forces of nature. Fujin, *kami* of wind, carries a large bag, and his companion *kami* of thunder, the menacing red-faced Raijin (or Raiden), holds a massive drum. Finally, a generic group of minor deities called *dosojin* have protected travelers ever since Izanagi brought them into being upon his return from the underworld. A *kami* called Koshin is one protector of travelers, but some also associate him with farming. His three monkey partners have become popular as "See no evil, hear no evil, do no evil." *Kami* keep watch over every conceivable feature of ordinary life. Suijin, for example, guards wells and other water sources, for water is the principal means of purification and an essential of life.

Two:

Development and Spread

13. If *Confucius* and *Laozi* were not considered divine early on, how did they come to assume so lofty a stature?

Very soon after Confucius's death, his followers initiated what would become a centuries-long process of elevating their teacher above the ranks of ordinary people. They revered him as a special ancestral figure, the pinnacle of wisdom. They built a temple in his honor in Qufu in 478 B.C.E. and, not long after that, began to enshrine statues and paintings of the Teacher and his major disciples there. Official imperial exaltation of Confucius did not begin until nearly five centuries after his death. After Han emperor Ping proclaimed Confucius the "Exalted Mount Ni Duke of Highest Perfection" in the year 1 C.E., a dozen other sovereigns followed the new tradition, bestowing similar accolades down to at least the sixteenth century. As early as the mid-fifth century C.E., the imperial authority dedicated a temple to Confucius, and within a century or two decreed state sponsored offerings in the Master's honor. Though Confucians have never considered Confucius divine, he has clearly ranked at the very zenith of human perfection. In keeping with the hierarchy of royal honorifics, the emperors decreed that Confucius would be known by such titles as Duke, First Teacher, First Sage, High King of Learning, and Ultimate Sage. Around 1530 C.E., emperors stopped using the language of royalty and switched to a set of titles designed to reflect wisdom rather than temporal power.

There seem to have been a number of stages in the process of Laozi's eventual deification. First, the legendary figure began as a teacher and writer, whose image eventually blended with that of the Yellow Emperor when Laozi came to be identified as a confidant of royalty. Traditional accounts such as the life-story summarized earlier transformed him into a culture hero whose mother had conceived him virginally. By the mid-second century C.E.,

Laozi had become the deity who delivered to Zhang Daoling the revelation of a new religious faith, giving rise to the Celestial Masters school. His image was still not complete. Next, perhaps also around the second or third century C.E., Laozi seems to have been identified as a creator god who also enters the world to rescue humanity from tribulation. Laozi was now capable of incarnating himself, almost like a Buddhist bodhisattva. Not long thereafter he joined the triad of the Three Pure Ones, and finally Laozi emerged as the chief divine person. We have here one of the more interesting examples of apotheosis, or deification, in the history of religion.

14. What *chief deities* and other important sacred personages eventually came to form the *Daoist pantheon?*

Bearing in mind that it is not always possible to draw neat distinctions between Daoist divinities and those of CCT, here are some of the figures that appear to have at least originated in Daoist circles. They are called the Earlier Heaven Deities. At the top of the pantheon are the Three Pure Ones *(San Qing)*. They seem to have been Daoism's theological rejoinder to the Buddhist groupings in which bodhisattvas flank Amitabha Buddha to form a celestial triad. The Three Pure Ones (or Sacred Beings) are named after the heavens in which they dwell: the heavens of the Jade, Higher, and Great Purity respectively. The triad evidently developed out of a trio of deified human beings of history or legend. Laozi, known as Tianshang Laojun (Lord of the Daoist Teaching), was the first so elevated. Later a deity called "Heavenly Venerable of the Original Beginning" (Yuanshi Tianzun) was named as chief deity. And still later a third deity, Grand Lord of the Dao (Taishang Daojun), leap-frogged the two others to the top of the triad. These three, often depicted as enthroned elders, came to be identified with the more transcendent and abstract Pure Ones. Many consider the deified Laozi still a separate deity who ranks above the Three Pure Ones. The Jade Emperor, Yuhuang

Dadi, was eventually identified either as the chief deity's younger brother or as an incarnation of the Lord of the Heaven of Great Purity, and became the prominent deity in some CCT cults. According to one theological model, the Three Pure Ones are manifestations of the primordial cosmic energy, *qi.*

There are in addition many other popular divine figures. One important subordinate deity is Xuantian Shangdi, Supreme Emperor of Dark Heaven. Jade Emperor dispatched him to earth to battle a band of renegade demon-kings. His iconography shows him enthroned and using a serpent and a turtle—leaders of the demons—as a footstool. Ruling the East is the divine consort of Xiwangmu (the Queen Mother of the West), Dung Wanggong, who lives in the remote magical fastness of the Kunlun mountains. In a reversal of the more usual dynamic, a "God of walls and moats," also known as the City God, began as a popular deity and made his way into the Daoist pantheon. During certain periods in history, the Heavenly Master appointed a given city's tutelary deity. The City God has the assistance of several other figures, called "spirit secretaries" in the idiom of public administration. They help the City God deliver his reports on the conduct of citizens to the authorities in Hell. Some other potent beings are clustered in groups. The Sen Nin are a group of sacred figures who dwell in heaven or in the distant misty mountains. Among the Sen Nin the most important are the Eight Immortals. Originally persons either historical (three) or legendary (five), they function as guardian figures of Daoism. Although they are not officially divine, popular lore sometimes attributes divine powers to them. They are called Later Heaven Deities, as are all human figures who eventually achieved immortality.

Many of the popular deities play multiple roles and sometimes resemble each other enough that one has to look carefully to identify them correctly. One of the most popular and frequently depicted deities is Guandi, often inaccurately characterized as the "war god" under the name Wudi. He was a third-century military leader named Guan Yu who gained a kind of martyr status after he was executed. By imperial decree in 1594, the deceased general was deified and the word for deity or emperor *(di)* added to his name. By a peculiar twist, he also acquired the status of secondary god of literature. Kuixing is the other secondary god of literature, distinguishable by his dragon-fish, writing brush and official seal, small stature, unpleasant countenance, and awkward one-legged stance. Many pray to him as they prepare for examinations. In popular belief, Kui elbowed out the principal deity of literature, Wenchang Dijun, who had actually begun his mythic life as a star deity who was then born as Changya, a famous literary figure. Wen generally wears a flowing robe and a large hat and is either enthroned or astride a mule. Kuixing usually stands on his left while on his right stands a red-coated figure named Chuyi.

15. How have Daoist/CCT history and myth come together in the stories of the *Jade Emperor, Guandi,* and the *Yellow Emperor?*

One of the more intriguing personalities in the Daoist and CCT pantheons is the Jade Emperor, Yuhuang Dadi. His emergence as a power to be reckoned with in popular worship offers important insight into the dynamics of Chinese religion generally. During the fifth and sixth centuries, Yuhuang Dadi was but one among many relatively minor deities. During the Tang dynasty of the seventh through ninth centuries, he gained prominence as a result of the appearance of a new text called the *Jade Emperor Scripture (Yuhuangjing)*. It tells how centuries earlier a queen had dreamt that Taishang Daojun, second of the Three Pure Ones, handed her an infant. She awoke and bore a child who after a short time as a young prince withdrew to mountain solitude. Lengthy spiritual discipline transformed the youth into the Jade Emperor. In the tenth century, a Song dynasty emperor named Jen Zung (r. 998–1022) chose Yuhuang Dadi as his patron deity and spread word of an expected revelation. That came in 1008 in the form of sacred scriptures, thus bolstering the weak emperor's position. Thereafter the Jade Emperor rose to the top of the popular pantheon, thus becoming the

CEO of a divine bureaucracy who runs a tight ship. Stories like that of the Jade Emperor help to explain why catalogues of the Daoist and CCT pantheons are sometimes a bit confusing.

Like the Jade Emperor, Guandi (also known as Guangong) claims a place in both Daoist and CCT pantheons. He has the additional distinction of ranking high in the upper echelons of the imperial cult, and through that channel connects with Confucian tradition as well. Guandi was originally a military man of the third century, named Guan Yu, who was executed after enemies of the Han dynasty captured him in battle. The court funded temples in his honor and publicized his cause. Meanwhile, the newly deified Guandi was gaining popularity among practitioners of CCT as a refuge from problems as diverse as illness, bad weather, and failing business. The ever-ready all-purpose deity thus rose to such prominence that his popular cult situates him above even the Jade Emperor. In the seventeenth century a Ming dynasty emperor conferred on Guandi the title Grand Emperor.

During the following regime, that of the Qing or Manchu, Guandi received the title under which he is perhaps most widely known, Military Emperor, Wudi, thus making him the official guardian of the empire. Guandi's celebrity represents a relatively recent development. Unlike many of the older deities, whose imagery and entourage were typically patterned on those of the imperial bureaucracy, Guandi is reminiscent of the Buddhist bodhisattva. In fact, some scholars suggest, Guandi was also absorbed into certain Buddhist groups after the seventh century. It seems likely that, as in the case of other indigenous Chinese deities, Guandi was first depicted under the general influence of Buddhism's use of sculpture. He appears as a very tall man with a long beard and a red face, sometimes accompanied by his son. Variant versions of his story give somewhat different details, as in the popular classic Chinese novel *Romance of the Three Kingdoms,* of which Guandi is the hero. Many popular theatrical presentations based on the novel have become major vehicles for the spread of Guandi's celebrity.

Ancient Chinese lore tells of Five August Emperors whose reigns date back to before 2500 B.C.E. They are sometimes called "culture heroes," in that tradition credits them with providing humankind with a host of skills and essential practical wisdom. As guardians of the five sacred mountains, the divine quintet ruled the cardinal directions and the center. Each was associated with a color: green with the east, red with the south, white with the west, black (or "dark") with the north, and yellow with the center. By far the most famous and popular of them is Huangdi, the Yellow Emperor, giver of such arts as medicine, agriculture, weaving, pottery, silkworm culture, and domestic architecture, to name only a few. Huangdi began his life in legend as a ruler and a shaman whose magical powers allowed him to confront all manner of evil. Dated to either 2697–2597 or 2674–2575 B.C.E., he was evidently a patron of the ancient *fangshi,* or shamans. But the Yellow Emperor went on to become one of the two patrons of an early Daoist school called Huanglao, perhaps a combination of the first names of Huangdi and Laozi. Huanglao Daoism may have begun as a religious movement as early as the third century B.C.E. In any case, though the figure of Laozi seems to have upstaged that of Huangdi for some centuries, the Yellow Emperor made a comeback in popularity. Walk into any number of Daoist and popular temples and you may encounter a statue of Huangdi prominently displayed, perhaps in his own glass case. Standing erect, the sovereign of solemn countenance wears elaborately embroidered robes whose main color is, of course, yellow.

16. What was the relationship between religious *ritual* and the power of the Chinese imperial court?

Ritual responsibilities of the emperor and his official delegates included ceremonies at various major state sacred sites, the Altar of the Spirits of Land and Grain, the Imperial Ancestral Temple, the temples of Heaven and Earth, of Sun and Moon, as well as within the audience halls of the Forbidden City. At the

Altar of the Spirits of Land and Grain *(she ji tan)* the emperor performed sacrifices in spring for fertile fields and in the fall for a plentiful harvest. At the Imperial Ancestral Temple *(tai miao),* he led ceremonies associated with the anniversaries of his own ancestors back through the history of the dynasty. There the ancestors were said to grant audiences with their royal public much as the emperor himself did from his own audience halls. At the Temple of Heaven, the imperial officials offered harvest prayers on New Year's day and rain prayers at the onset of summer, and announced royal events such as the designation of the heir to the throne. Within the Forbidden City, various important rituals occurred at the new year, the winter solstice, and on the emperor's birthday. Subjects acknowledged the emperor's lofty authority in the various audience halls of the City's outer court, located just south of the more private palaces of the inner court. The ceremony began early in the morning outside the Meridian Gate, the southern entrance to the Forbidden City. At the sound of two drum beats, three thousand officials in nine ranks processed into the courtyard before the Hall of Supreme Harmony. Once they were arranged, three drum beats announced that the emperor would enter from the Hall of Middle Harmony just to the north and take his seat on the throne. Music accompanied his entry and continued as all the officials paid homage. Military leaders lined up on the west and civil authorities on the east, both groups facing the central axis of the courtyard. Bird and animal symbolism was arranged on the robes so that the birds and animals of both groups were facing north, honoring the emperor as he sat on the dragon throne within the hall. All of creation was thus symbolically ordered toward the emperor, who represented Heaven. After the formal announcement of the specific occasion for the ritual, music resumed for another round of obeisance to the emperor. Once the emperor had departed, the ceremony ended with an exit procession of all present.

CIT rituals were arranged in a symbolic hierarchical order that coordinated the authority of those performing the rituals with the various ranks of the CIT pantheon. To symbolize universal dominion, the emperor would make offerings to the powers controlling all four cardinal directions and to all mountains and rivers, as well as the "five domestic sacrifices." On lower levels, ritual responsibilities reflected a division of labor and authority. Imperial princes made offerings only to the power ruling their own quarters of the universe and associated mountains and rivers, and the five domestic sacrifices. These took place at regional sacred sites. The princes' chief officers in turn were to perform only the domestic offerings, and their subordinates only the offerings to their own ancestors. These last rituals occurred in home settings and in cemeteries. Specific rituals included many of the same kinds of actions Daoists or practitioners of CCT might engage in. Ritual specialists generally purified themselves for the ceremonies by fasting and ablutions. Prior to offerings to divine powers of the top level in the pantheon, specialists fasted for three days, and for second level deities, two days. During times of fasting, ritualists were especially careful to avoid certain strong foods (garlic and onions) and fermented beverages. An essential ingredient in the preparatory period was avoidance of contact with death and disease. Festivities and music were put aside. Central to the actual worship ceremonies was the offering of food, wine, and incense, along with prayers of petition and physical prostration before the deities.

17. Have the Chinese traditions ever been intimately identified with specific *political regimes,* the way Shinto became Japan's "national" creed?

Confucianism: Confucian teaching offers a great deal of reflection on the nature of an orderly society and methods of governing. It is therefore not surprising that a number of political regimes have chosen the Confucian system as their official ideology. Emperor Wudi (r. 140–87 B.C.E.) of the Han dynasty (206 B.C.E.–220 C.E.) was the first to do so, paving the way for a long

Hall of Harvest Prayer at the northern end of the sprawling complex of the Altar (Temple) of Heaven, Beijing, set on a circular, three-tiered platform. Here the emperor performed sacred rites at prescribed times.

and complex association between Confucian teaching and Chinese government. In Korea, Confucianism became the official religion of Korea by decree of the Yi (1392–1910) dynasty in 1392, to Buddhism's detriment. Leaders condemned Buddhism's view of this world as illusory and argued for the Confucian tradition's more humanistic approach. Perhaps the single most far-reaching result was that education toppled from its elite pedestal and became available to a wide public. Confucianism took somewhat longer to forge its links to the Japanese imperial government. During the Tokugawa period (1600–1867), after the capital had moved to Tokyo, Confucian tradition enjoyed its closest association with Japanese imperial rule. The legacy of Confucian political thought stood out particularly in the realm of international relations. Confucians played an important role in the Meiji Restoration of 1868, which involved a restructuring of imperial administration. As the Japanese grew to regard Confucianism as an unwelcome import, the tradition's official influence in governmental circles diminished steadily.

Daoism: During several periods of Chinese history, Daoism has enjoyed the considerable benefits of imperial patronage. One Daoist emperor in particular, during the mid-ninth century, launched a devastating persecution of Buddhism that did serious damage to many of that tradition's monasteries and temples. There is a certain irony in that, given the classical Daoist teaching about law and government. According to the *Daodejing* and *Zhuangzi,* the best hope for society is unobtrusive leadership that does not need to rely on law and force to lead. Governmental institutions are meddlesome and oppressive. According to early Daoist authorities, the ideal social setting is the small village in which no one carries weapons. Very unlike classical Confucian tradition in this respect, the ideal Daoist society does away with social stratification of all kinds. Where all are equal, ruling and military classes are unnecessary. Throughout Chinese history, however, Daoists and Confucians competed with one another for imperial support and patronage. Confucianism has generally been far more closely identified with government than has Daoism. Despite classical Daoist aversion to formal structures of government, both the official and popular pantheons retained a good deal of the imagery of imperial bureaucracy, as in the names of such deities as the Jade Emperor.

18. Is there a distinctively *Confucian interpretation of history?*

Confucius refused to think of himself as an innovator. Any individual bent on inventing his own system of thought was doomed to failure, so interdependent are we humans. His task, he believed, was what he called the "renewal of antiquity." His first step was to translate his knowledge of tradition into clearly articulated principles so that he could intelligently sort out the best of the past. Confucius discerned in the drift of history a serious problem of societal entropy—the tendency to let things unravel. Looking back to the legendary founders of Chinese society, Confucius believed the first major problem set in when the Xia dynasty (1994–1525 B.C.E.) instituted the principle of hereditary succession. When the quality of the rulers had declined to a disastrous low, the Shang dynasty (1525–1028 B.C.E.) overthrew the last Xia tyrant. Unfortunately, the Shang rulers retained the hereditary throne, thus virtually sealing their own eventual demise. Sure enough, the Zhou dynasty (1040–256 B.C.E.) was destined to be the instrument of renewal. By Confucius's own time, the Zhou, too, showed signs of serious decay. The Master wondered what power under Heaven might again correct the course of history. Confucius was convinced that it was possible to imitate the eternally true in history, to avoid reliving all of the past by distinguishing the good from the evil in it. True authority arose out of the ability to blend the ancient with the new. And only through learning could a leader assimilate the eternally true to changing needs. Beginning with politics and ethics, Confucius set out to contribute to the renewal of antiquity.

19. Have there been any important Confucian *reform movements?* What are *Neo-Confucianism* and *Neo-Daoism?*

Wang Yangming (1472–1529 C.E.) was an outspoken government official of the Ming dynasty. He was perhaps the most influential teacher of the neo-Confucian School of Mind, also known as the Idealists (Xinxue). Wang believed that the teaching of his predecessors in the neo-Confucian movement had lost all credibility when Yuan dynasty (1280–1368) bureaucrats made it the official curriculum for civil service examinations. Reduced to a fixed set of questions and answers, neo-Confucian ideas no longer required people to think independently. Wang's major work, *Investigation into the "Great Learning,"* commented on the ancient Confucian text, underscoring the need for active engagement with ideas. He condemned slavish adherence to rigid canons of ritual propriety. Wang argued for an understanding of *li* as a living universal principle rather than a list of prescribed procedures and policies. He borrowed from Daoist and Buddhist teachings, as earlier neo-Confucians had done, attempting to reinvigorate the tradition as a way of interpreting the whole of life. And Wang reintroduced a metaphysical element by speaking of a "true self" and a "heavenly principle." Above all, he insisted, one must not lose sight of the underlying challenge of human development and the struggle for moral improvement. Institutionalize what is meant to be a living tradition, Wang warned, and you create a giant fossil.

During the Song Dynasty (960–1279 C.E.), Confucian tradition underwent a kind of renaissance. Buddhism and Daoism had both developed into powerful influences at all levels of Chinese life and culture. A host of talented Confucian scholars reinterpreted their tradition in light of, and in "dialogue" with, Buddhist and Daoist concepts. Three tenth- and eleventh-century scholars pioneered what has come to be known in China as the School of Principle (Lixue) and beyond Asia as Neo-Confucianism. Sun Fu (922–1057), Shi Qia (1005–1045), and Hu Yuan (933–1059) transformed and revitalized the Confucian curriculum, thus paving the way for later teachers in their movement. Zhou Dunyi (1017–1073) continued the dramatic changes by developing *li* as a spiritual or metaphysical principle rather than simply a term for propriety in relationships and ritual. He and his successors expanded Confucian teaching into a full-scale cosmological system. Zhuxi (1130–1200) is the "Thomas Aquinas" of the school in the sense that he synthesized the teachings of his predecessors into his own carefully coordinated system. Zhuxi became a sort of lightning rod for subsequent generations of scholars, all of whom had to account for his pioneering thought one way or another.

Neo-Daoism is a name commonly given to various developments around the third and fourth centuries C.E. Some scholars suggest that there were two recognizable schools. One was called Secret Mystical Teaching (Xuanxue). According to some interpreters, an important theme was its emphasis on the quest for physical immortality. Earlier Daoist sources had spoken of immortality, but generally of the spiritual rather than the bodily sort. Neo-Daoism recommended exercises in breathing, diet, use of potions, elixirs, and talismans, and sexual activity reminiscent of Hindu and Buddhist Tantric practices. But perhaps more fundamental to this alchemy were intense meditative practices intended to reveal the Dao within the individual. A major feature of the second school, known as Pure Conversation (Qingtan), is its attempt to blend aspects of Daoist, Confucian, and Buddhist thought. Among its proponents were the so-called Seven Sages of the Bamboo Grove, whose penchant for detached philosophical discourse and the cultivation of a Daoist aesthetic were among their hallmarks. On the basis of their reading of the *Zhuangzi* and *Daodejing,* they developed a Neo-Daoist interpretation of the so-called Confucian classics. After the fifth century, Buddhist concepts infiltrated the movement to such a degree that Neo-Daoism gradually lost its distinctiveness and identity.

20. What is the historical importance of the developments known as *Dual Shinto* and the *School of National Learning?*

Dual (or *ryobu,* "two-sided") Shinto arose out of the early interaction between Shinto theology and Buddhist thinking newly imported from China. Some use the term *ryobu shugo,* "dual compromise," to describe the resulting syncretism. A number of accounts describe the developments this way. In 715 C.E. a Shinto shrine annexed a Buddhist temple to itself. Twenty years later a smallpox epidemic created a crisis situation to which the emperor responded by commissioning the colossal Great Buddha *(daibutsu)* at Nara's Todaiji (Eastern Great Temple). At the same time, the ruler dispatched the Buddhist patriarch Gyogi to Ise shrine to seek the blessing of Amaterasu, the Shinto sun goddess. Gyogi secured a favorable oracle, and the next night the emperor had a dream in which Amaterasu identified herself as the Mahayana Buddha of Infinite Light, Vairocana. This laid the groundwork for further identification of the various *kami* as alter-egos of various Buddhas and bodhisattvas. In 750, an image of the Shinto war *kami* Hachiman was transported from its shrine at Usa on the island of Kyushu (just south of the main Japanese island, Honshu) to Todaiji in Nara so that the *kami* might pay respects to the Daibutsu. Hachiman thereafter remained in a special shrine at Todaiji where he became the guardian *kami* of Todaiji. Thus did a Shinto *kami* come to protect the teachings of the Buddha. This account reflects an interpretation devised during the ninth century by teachers of a new esoteric school of Buddhism called Shingon. As always, this theological accommodation had its political implications and set the stage for many years of Buddhist growth and royal patronage. From then until 1868, Dual Shinto was the dominant form of Shinto. With the Meiji Restoration of imperial power came increasing pressure from Shinto scholars to purge the tradition of all Chinese influences, including of course Buddhism and Confucianism, both of which had by turns exerted considerable pull at court for centuries.

"National Learning" or Kokugaku had perhaps more to do with the modern understanding of Shinto than any other movement within the tradition. Kada no Azumamaro (1669–1736), generally considered the founder of the school, insisted on the need to return to the earliest genuinely and purely Japanese sources. Among those he included the *Kujiki,* but emphasized the *Kojiki* and *Nihongi* especially. Kamo no Mabuchi (1697–1769) continued what Kada had begun by applying philological methods to classical Japanese prayer and poetry. Spontaneity he considered the native Japanese gift, without which nothing could be truly Japanese. Motoori Norinaga (1730–1801) continued the scholarly dynasty and is still regarded by some as Shinto's best theological mind. His forty-four volume commentary on the *Kojiki* remains a monument of scholarship. Hirata Atsutane (1763–1843) was the latest and perhaps most influential exponent of the school in that he implemented the thought of his predecessor Motoori. Together these four men were largely responsible for the articulation of modern Shinto's highly nationalistic and ethnocentric tone.

21. How would you sum up the *history of Confucianism?*

During the first couple of centuries after the time of Confucius, two major thinkers developed the beginnings of what we now call Confucianism. Mencius, or Mengzi (372–289 B.C.E.), and Xunzi (d. 215 B.C.E.) codified the teachings of the Master into the foundations of a political philosophy. Emperor Qin Shihuangdi (221–210 B.C.E.), displeased with the emerging movement, tried to suppress it by burning all the Confucian texts. Before that emperor died, in 210 B.C.E., he had succeeded in transforming feudal China into a centralized bureaucracy, but Confucianism survived. Under the new Han dynasty (206 B.C.E.–220 C.E.) the state espoused Confucianism as its core ideology. Confucianism took institutional shape as a system for training the empire's bureaucrats and officials, thereby strengthening the cultural elite known as the Literati. For the next several centuries, Confucianism's prestige dwindled as Buddhism's star rose with increasing imperial patronage.

During the Southern and Northern (265–581 C.E.), Sui (581–618), and Tang dynasties (618–906) Confucian ritual and Literati authority held on, criticizing Buddhism as an insidious import and enjoying sporadic periods of notoriety. Confucianism returned to prominence during the Song dynasty (960–1279) as a result of the Neo-Confucian revival. Scholars finalized the Canon of the Five Classics and Four Books, plus several subsidiary works. Official Neo-Confucian philosophies drifted away from traditional beliefs in a transcendent divine Heaven, emphasizing ethics and social responsibility. But a cult centered around Confucius survived. During the last of the Chinese dynasties, the Qing or Manchu (1644–1912), a generally strong Literati class continued to promote an increasingly static and dogmatic form of Confucian "orthodoxy."

The last emperor fell with the arrival of Sun Yat Sen's new Republic and the Literati became functionally obsolete. Still, the leaders of the Republic held Confucius up as the epitome of Chinese culture. When Maozi Dong's Communist movement began its rise in the 1930s, the Chairman declared himself fed up with Confucius and the old ways. In response, the Republican-Nationalist movement insisted that Confucianism represented all genuinely Chinese values. As the Nationalists fled the mainland and established themselves in Taiwan under Zhang Gaishek in 1949, overt acknowledgment of Confucian tradition went with them.

22. How would you summarize the *history of religious Daoism?*

Here is truly a story of ups and downs. Religious Daoism emerged as a recognizable tradition in its own right during the latter decades of the Han dynasty (206 B.C.E.–220 C.E.). Confucianism enjoyed imperial favor as the official creed of the state. But when the Han dynasty disintegrated, both Daoism and Buddhism found room to grow. The early Celestial Masters school dominated the Daoist scene for the most part. Various schools teaching forms of alchemical Daoism developed early on and have continued throughout the past two thousand years. In addition, new revelations claimed by various teachers gave rise to several new schools between the third and sixth centuries, times of political fragmentation. With political reunification during the Sui (581–618) dynasty, Daoism's various schools managed to survive in spite of meager imperial support. Monasteries generally flourished but remained apart from the general populace. But things improved under the Tang dynasty (618–906) when Daoists once again had friends in high places.

Under the Song dynasty (960–1279), Neo-Confucianism proved a powerful rival for Daoists at court. But Daoists fared well anyway, since many Neo-Confucians gladly exchanged ideas with Daoism's leading lights. During the Southern Song dynasty (1127–1279), in spite of an almost complete lack of public imperial patronage, several new Daoist schools sprang up. Things took a turn for the worse under the Yuan (1260–1368) or Mongol dynasty. Daoists invited to participate in court debates suffered serious setbacks and paid dearly with the loss of monasteries and precious libraries. During the late medieval Ming dynasty (1368–1644), Daoist fortunes improved again dramatically and many Daoist masters enjoyed prominent official positions. But under the last of the imperial regimes, the Qing (or Manchu) dynasty (1644–1912), the pendulum swung the other way and religious Daoism struggled to survive the early modern period.

Through the periods of the first Chinese Republic (1912–1949) and the People's Republic (1949 to present), Daoism has held on largely thanks to the establishment of several organizations designed to provide a public presence for the various orders and schools. After disastrous losses as a result of the Cultural Revolution (1966–1976), Daoist religious groups are again struggling to pull themselves back together.

23. How would you sum up the *history of Shinto?*

Beliefs now associated with the religious tradition called Shinto originated long before anyone ever referred to them as "the way of the *kami.*" Archaeological evidence points to various forms of nature worship, ancestor veneration, shamanistic rituals, and animistic beliefs in an agricultural society during the neolithic (7000–2500 B.C.E.) and bronze-iron (2500–1000 B.C.E.) ages. Primitive shrines dedicated to the community or clan deities called *ujigami* appeared between 100 and 552 C.E. Sometime in the later sixth century C.E., after the arrival of Butsu-do or the "Way of the Buddha," Japanese distinguished indigenous beliefs from the imported tradition by inventing a name for it. During the Nara period (710–784), the Nakatomi clan served as priests of a nascent imperial Shinto whose earliest major shrines were those of Ise and Izumo.

By 737 Shinto shrines numbered over three thousand, one out of four enjoying direct government support. In the first capital, Nara, the Fujiwara clan founded the important Kasuga shrine. Kasuga was destined to play a critical role in the development of a hybrid of Buddhism and Shinto through its relationship with the nearby Buddhist temple of Todaiji. Throughout the Heian period (794–1185), with the capital newly established at Kyoto, Shinto's fortunes were intimately bound up with developments in Buddhism. Theologians on both sides devised theories designed to fit the two belief systems together, thereby inventing Dual Shinto, a blend of both Shinto and Buddhist elements.

The Kamakura period (1185–1333) witnessed the rise of feudal lords *(daimyo)* and a *samurai* warrior caste under a *shogun* ("throne field marshal") of the Minamoto family, which had toppled the Fujiwara clan. The samurai code was called *bushido* ("way of the warrior"), a blend of Confucian aristocratic conservatism, Buddhist mental discipline, and Shinto patriotism. Under the Minamoto, the two chief *kami* were Sugawara Michizane, patron of literary and social concerns, and Hachiman, *kami* of war. Shinto grew as a popular religious tradition during the Muromachi/Ashikaga period (1333–1568, first name referring to the capital outside Kyoto and the second to the clan in power) with imperial patronage of pilgrimage to Ise shrine.

Pre- and early modern developments during the Momoyama/Azuchi (1568–1615) and Edo/Tokugawa periods (1615–1867) included Shinto's steady ascendancy over Buddhism and identification with the political power of dictatorial shoguns. Eighteenth- and nineteenth-century Japanese isolationism went hand in hand with attempts to rid Shinto of foreign elements. That culminated in the Meiji Reform, ushering in the modern period (1868–1945) and restoring the emperor to divine status. World War II called Shinto's imperial theology into question and saw a return of popular sectarian movements.

THREE:

DOCTRINES AND PRACTICES

24. Is *creed* an important concept in the major Chinese and Japanese traditions?

Confucianism/CIT: Neither Confucianism as such nor the CIT have ever formulated a specific creedal statement to which all members are expected to confess their allegiance. If asked to summarize his or her religious beliefs, a devout and well-informed Chinese man or woman of a century or two ago would likely have included a number of basic elements relating to Confucianism and the CIT. Divine Heaven rules all things through a "mandate" made known to a "Son of Heaven" called the emperor. The emperor in turn governs all earthly affairs by enacting that mandate, whose hallmark is justice and equity. It is the emperor's duty to make timely and appropriate offerings to Heaven and Earth to ensure the felicitous coordination of all cosmic events for the benefit of humankind. Confucius, as one of the sages, represents a revered tradition of practical wisdom to which a sincere emperor subscribes. All good subjects, too, will acknowledge the sage and those of his stature and will venerate them along with their own ancestors. All of this, they might add, fits into the larger picture of the ultimate harmony represented by the balance of all things under the power of the Dao, which is manifest in Heaven and Earth.

Daoism/CCT: Since religious Daoism and CCT emphasize practice over correct belief, they have not formulated the equivalent of creedal summaries such as those of Judaism and Islam, or even Buddhism. Daoism and CCT do, of course, presuppose certain basic beliefs and assumptions about how the world works. Most of those beliefs have to do with discerning and understanding how to cope with and benefit from the spiritual forces inherent in all things. All of the varieties of religious Daoism and CCT, therefore, have their core beliefs. But affirming one's assent to

47

them pales in insignificance compared to the importance of grasping the essential skills needed to negotiate life's daily challenges.

Shinto: Shinto beliefs, like those of Daoism and CCT, have never been reduced to a concise formal summary statement. If one were to produce a brief Shinto creedal affirmation it might go something like this: I believe that sacredness surrounds me, that it pervades all things including my very self, and that the all-suffusing divine presence is ultimately benevolent and meant to assure well-being and happiness for all who acknowledge it and strive to live in harmony with it. Shortly after the Meiji Restoration in 1868, the imperial authorities formulated the rough equivalent of a brief creedal statement, called the Three Great Teachings, in an attempt to enhance the emperor's status. The three teachings included patriotism and respect for the *kami,* establishing heavenly principles in relation to human culture, and dedication to the emperor and his pronouncements. Authorities interpreted the creed in the context of worship of the sun goddess, Amaterasu, and the other chief deities in the creation myth. Though it approximated a creed in some ways, this "official" statement was more like an acknowledgment of the importance of underlying religious conviction for the good order of Japanese society.

25. Are *"doctrine"* and *"dogma"* important concepts in Chinese and Japanese religion?

Confucianism/CIT: Ancient tradition gave the generic name *Rujia,* the "Teaching of the Scholars," to a way of thinking and performing rituals that predated Confucius. Confucius inherited the way of that imperial cult, which included elaborate sacrificial ceremonies addressed to Heaven and Earth as part of the overall worldview of *"Yin* and *Yang."* According to that view, all things are composed of varying proportions of the female principle, *Yin,* characterized as dark, moist, and associated with valleys; and the male principle, *Yang,* characterized as bright, dry, and associated with mountain peaks. After Confucius's time, the Great Teacher's interpretation of that traditional heritage came to be known as the "Teaching of Confucius" *(Kongjia)*. Throughout the long histories of both Confucianism and the CIT, Chinese have been aware of various elements in their teaching that in effect comprise a body of doctrine. Rarely, if ever, has either Confucianism or the CIT shown any tendency toward dogmatic pronouncements meant as a litmus test by which to measure the allegiance of the public. Some scholars talk of a kind of orthodoxy in the Neo-Confucian schools of the Song and later dynasties. But in general a broad acceptance of a core body of teachings has simply been presumed.

Daoism/CCT: Most of the various schools and sects of Daoism can point to at least one source or compendium of their central teachings. In that sense, there is such a thing as Daoist doctrine. A "body" of doctrine does in effect define the boundaries of some of the schools, especially the more esoteric ones, and sets them apart. But even in those instances, the doctrinal core is largely subordinate to a given school's central rituals and practices. CCT, on the other hand, does not define itself according to any clearly articulated doctrinal system. Children learn from their parents and extended family of elders a host of convictions and practices of the sort often called "folk beliefs." Where there is no formally defined doctrine, there can be no dogma in the sense of a minimum required for membership. Of those Daoist schools and sects that have developed distinctive doctrinal tenets, only the most esoteric have approached anything like the kind of official dogmatic pronouncement one finds, for example, in Roman Catholicism.

Shinto: Shinto has been influential in Japanese life through a relatively small number of specific and well-defined beliefs. Ancient tradition teaches the sacredness of nature, and of the existence of specific individual and personal divine beings, including those mentioned in the myth as well as a number of others. Some of those divine beings have had universal importance throughout Japan and the history of Shinto. Others have been of more regional or local importance. The teaching with perhaps the farthest reaching cultural implications is that of the divine ancestry of the emperor. Other significant elements of the myth that one could call doctrinal have to do with the divine origins of Japan itself and with the essential need of ritual purity. Across Japan and over the centuries, many other doctrine-like features have been important, but Shinto has never been a dogmatic tradition in that it has not explicitly made adherence to a specific set of doctrines a standard for membership in the community of believers. Far more significant has been the standard of participation in community through its vast complex of ritual practices. Those rituals are in turn deeply rooted in the primal myth.

26. Is the concept of *revelation* useful in understanding the traditions of China and Japan?

Confucianism/CIT: Confucianism is very different from traditions like the Abrahamic faiths, with their scriptures believed to have been revealed by a transcendent deity through prophetic messengers. It is different from Hinduism as well, a tradition that revolves around sacred texts. But Hinduism's scriptures are not so much directly revealed as they are disclosed timelessly to those sages and seers with the sensitivity to discern the eternal truths. Confucians think of their central truths as sacred, but not as either revealed from on high or disclosed from below. They are the records of the great sages and scholars that enshrine the highest insights into human nature and preserve the bedrock of China's ritual and literary patrimony. The CIT understanding of the emperor's responsibility to maintain contact with the Will of Heaven may sound at first like a variation on the theme of revelation. But in this case the Heavenly Mandate remains rather vague and amorphous, a cosmic truth for which the Son of Heaven must cultivate a refined sensitivity.

Daoism/CCT: Most Daoist sects and schools, and CCT generally, teach that religious truths are embedded in virtually all levels and facets of reality. Access to those truths is available largely through the mediation of qualified ritual specialists and spiritual masters. Their task is not so much to disclose the mysteries as to facilitate the passage of power from the realm of gods and spirits to that of human beings. When ordinary people find themselves in the neighborhood of these spiritual powers, the truth behind them remains mysterious and cloaked in ambiguity. There are, however, accounts in which famous masters and sages claim to have received explicit revelations or missions directly from a deity. When Daoists talk the language of revelation in those relatively rare instances, they suggest that they are pointing only to the tip of the iceberg, so to speak. The whole truth remains hidden from view and available only to a select few. This contrasts markedly with the general thrust of the Abrahamic traditions, for example, where revelation implies the disclosure of the full truth insofar as human beings can fathom it. Finally, an experience called "divination writing" deserves mention here, since it is occasionally described as a revelatory medium. The Shangqing school claims to be based on a series of nocturnal revelations. Founder Yang Xi reports that heavenly beings came to him in a vision and caused his hand to write the sacred texts.

Shinto: All religious traditions are oriented in varying degrees to two great inseparable realities—truth and power. Some, such as the Abrahamic traditions, Judaism, Christianity, and Islam, tend to tilt slightly toward truths of the kind human beings cannot access without direct help from the source of truth itself. Others, such as Daoism, focus more on teaching believers how to discern and benefit from the wellsprings of power. Shinto is far more concerned with power than with truth. This is obviously an oversimplification. What it means is that the power of the divine and its implications are the only important truths. Where and how do human beings have access to those truths? Preeminently through the marvels of nature, including the human. Shinto's deities do not reveal a message otherwise inaccessible to mortals, as is the case in the Abrahamic faiths, for example. They do, however, disclose all the truth human beings need to anyone who reflects on his or her life with a clear mind and heart.

27. Does belief in an *afterlife* play an important role in Chinese and Japanese religious thought?

Confucianism/CIT: Confucius did not focus on life after death as though it were the ultimate standard against which to measure the success of a life on earth. With the majority of his fellow Chinese, the Teacher shared the conviction that biological death did not signal a definitive end to life. Death did not mean annihilation and loss in some great void beyond the grave. Confucius clearly believed in some form of spiritual survival, and in the ongoing presence of those who have departed this life. But like the Buddha, Confucius and his disciples chose not to speculate about possible celestial or infernal post-mortem scenarios. Daoism and CCT would offer ample options in that regard. Confucius neither denied nor affirmed any particular views. He was convinced that human beings understood far too little of life here and now to waste it planning for a hereafter they understood even less. When classical Confucian sources talk about Heaven, therefore, they do not have in mind anything like a realm of eternal reward for those who die in a state of righteousness. Heaven is merely a name for the highest spiritual presence of which human beings are aware.

Daoism/CCT: Since long before the beginnings of religious Daoism, the notion of Heaven *(tian)* as an impersonal transcendent reality has been very important to the Chinese. Some Daoists have identified Heaven as the first materialization, a kind of emanation, of the Dao's spiritual power. In this sense, Heaven becomes an intermediary between the unmanifest Dao and all of creation, for Heaven is the source of all good things. Along with Earth and Humanity, Heaven is one of the "three powers" that make life as we know it happen. However, Daoists do not generally talk of Heaven as the eternal abode of those who lived virtuously on earth. One image of a region beyond ordinary earthly experience is called the Isles of the Blest *(Penglai Shan)* in the far reaches of the Eastern Sea, where the Eight Immortals dwell amid an idyllic landscape. Many Chinese express the hope of finally reaching the Isles and there attaining immortality.

Belief in retribution after death for a less-than-praiseworthy life has given rise to a wealth of imagery. Both Daoism and CCT call Hell a multi-storied "earthly prison." There are ten levels of hell—some prefer to talk of ten separate hells—each with its ruling deity. They function rather like the circles of hell in Dante's *Inferno,* each designated for those who commit specific sins and crimes. Presiding over the first level is a sort of chief judge who wields authority over the other nine judge-kings. Some souls never make it to their assigned hell, a difficult passageway to the hope of better things beyond that. They spend eternity wandering aimlessly and forever hungry, dependent on the kindness of the living to attend to their needs. Certain sources talk of hell much as many Christians describe purgatory, temporary suffering with long-range benefits.

Shinto: Ancient traditions tell of another world, a realm beyond this one, called the High Plain of Heaven *(takama no hara).* It is a happy state, heaven *(ame),* a spiritual land connected to earth by a wondrous bridge. That mythic realm overflows with life and fecundity *(tokoyo no kuni).* Devout worshipers call the *kami* down, recalling how they descended before time began to bring the sacred land and its people into existence. There is also a netherworld, a most unpleasant state called the Land of Darkness *(yomi no kuni).* Ruled by death, that land is filled with wretched pollution and impurity. To that land worshipers dispatch troublesome spirits and hope their own prayers and attentiveness to the rites of ancestor veneration will keep the negative forces at bay. Most people today do not believe that the dead end up in one or other of the realms beyond this world. Nevertheless, certain fundamental criteria determine whether an individual spirit will be content or disgruntled after death. Those include the ethical quality of one's life and one's attentiveness to avoiding impurity attached to taboo behavior. Some speak simply of a "world beyond view" *(kakuriyo),* an otherwise non-descript state of being after this life.

28. Are *salvation* or *redemption* important concepts?

Confucianism/CIT: According to a prevailing classical Chinese view of human nature, people are naturally capable of choosing either good or evil. A central concept in Confucian teaching is that each human being has the innate capacity for moral improvement. Confucius's successor Mengzi took the Master's teaching a step further, for he was convinced that human beings were essentially good and naturally inclined to ethical betterment. Even the more skeptical Xunzi, who held that individuals were born with a proclivity for self-centeredness, allowed that proper education could turn a person around. Individuals who choose to act selfishly hurt themselves and their fellow human beings, but their choices do not in any way damage a divine-human relationship as some traditions teach. People are capable of righting the wrongs they commit if they are willing to face the responsibility of setting neglected or sabotaged relationships right. This includes all relationships. Given that, Confucian tradition has no need for notions like salvation or redemption. It does not talk of savior or redeemer figures, but of moral leaders who teach by example, much the way classical Theravada Buddhism speaks of the Buddha.

Daoism/CCT: Some elements in Daoist tradition talk a great deal about a type of salvation from mortality itself. That is quite different from the kind of salvation Muslims and Christians look forward to, something closer to salvation in spite of mortality. For Daoists, the most spiritually accomplished individuals are capable of so purifying themselves that they can actually live on eternally in the Paradise of Immortals. They might appear to die and be buried, but only because they allowed that to happen as a concession to widespread belief and socially acceptable convention. In fact, they are able to substitute something else for their body and slip away unnoticed to paradise. What about ordinary folks incapable of such lofty feats? They can still hope to receive an immortal body after resurrection, a belief with some similarity to classic Christian notions of bodily resurrection. Another important distinction between Daoist notions of salvation and, for example, Christian beliefs, is that there is no single savior figure in Daoist thought.

Shinto: Salvation is not a question of deliverance from the present human condition into a realm beyond. Shinto tradition teaches that the solution to the human predicament is just the reverse: sincere worshipers welcome the *kami* into the world of everyday concerns. Salvation therefore means sacralizing the ordinary so that life here and now becomes the best it can be.

29. What kind of *ritual calendar* do these traditions observe?

Chinese: Whether Daoist, CCT, Buddhist, or Confucian, all Chinese have historically acknowledged the same overall reckoning of time. Official Confucian and CIT events were traditionally set by a Board of Astrology and promulgated by a Ministry of Rites. Firmly anchored in traditional astrological calculations, the Chinese lunar calendar consists of twelve months of twenty-nine or thirty days, since the time between new moons is about twenty-nine and a half days. The lunar year dovetails with the solar with the insertion of an extra month approximately every six years, or when five additional days per year total thirty. Reckoning began around 2637 B.C.E., so that the year 2000 marks the year 4637. Each of the twelve animals of the zodiac is associated with a particular quality or event and gives its name to every twelfth year, beginning with the Rat (industry and prosperity) and proceeding in order through Ox (spring planting), Tiger (valor), Hare (longevity), Dragon (power and good fortune), Snake (cunning), Horse (perseverance), Sheep (filial piety) or Goat, Monkey (health), Rooster (protection), Dog (fidelity), and Pig (home and family). The year 2000 is the Year of the Dragon, 2001 that of the Snake, 2002 that of the Horse, and so on. Five full cycles, each named after one of the five elements (wood, fire, earth, metal, and water) equals sixty years, an important interval for ritual purposes. Major annual markers are the winter (maximum Yin) and summer (maximum Yang) solstices and vernal and autumnal equinoxes when Yin and Yang are in balance. During each month, the most important times are the moments of new and full moon.

Each month is divided into ten-day periods, six of those in turn considered a special time period, and six of those in turn equaling a full year. In addition, each year is divided into twenty-four climatic periods called breaths or nodes, described by such phrases as "full of snow" or "clear and bright." Every year, month, day, and hour is further identified by a combination of ten heavenly "stems" and twelve earthly "branches" (the monthly or zodiacal symbols). The ten heavenly stems are associated with colors, two stems with each of the five symbolic colors (azure, red, yellow, white, black), which are in turn linked to the four directions and center as well as to the five elements. Branches and stems are both primarily numerical designators, but each also bears important symbolic connotations. If you match one stem with one branch for succeeding years (S1/B1, S2/B2...S1/B11, S2/B12, S3/B1, and so on), you end up back at the beginning after sixty years. In this system, only odd-numbered stems combine with odd-numbered branches, even numbered with even numbered. We are currently in the sixty-year cycle that began in 1984.

The result of all this calculation is an extremely detailed system of pinpointing special times according to a host of definitive characteristics. Each event occurring on earth has its heavenly parallel. The calendar has been not merely a way of keeping track of times for religious observances, but a kind of temporal map for negotiating the cosmos as well. Each year, during the ninth lunar month, imperial officials formerly set up the liturgical calendar for the year to come.

Japanese: Shinto reckoning of ritual time has been much influenced by Chinese traditions. As early as 675 C.E., religious Daoism had made a significant impact on the Japanese imperial court, which formally adopted many Daoist practices. Most important, the court set up a special bureau of divination based on Daoist principles, called the Onmyoryo ("Office of Yin-Yang"). One of the Onmyoryo's chief functions was to establish a liturgical calendar that patterned earthly life on the rhythms of the cosmos. This lunar calendar retains all the main features of its Chinese model, including the cycles of sixty years based on the combinations of twelve "branches" and ten "stems." The Japanese call their Chinese version of the lunar calendar *"Kyureki,"* as distinct from the modern solar calendar adopted in 1872, the *"Shinreki."* An early formal cycle of annual observance, called the *nenchu gyoji,* literally "year-round-discipline-rituals," developed as early as the tenth century C.E. Imperial authorities promulgated it in a vast historical record called the *Engishiki (Institutes of the Engi Era,* 901–923 C.E.), an essential source of information about Shinto ritual in general. Japan's lunar calendar needs to tuck in an extra month every three years or so. Prior to the nineteenth century, many Shinto shrines maintained their own calendars of events, including uniquely regional and local festivities. Today some major events still take place according to various ways of adapting the lunar calendar to fit the solar. For example, some festivals now occur on the same numbered day within the same numbered month, but transferred to the solar reckoning. In other words, a festival that fell on the seventh day of the seventh lunar month now falls on July 7. Some festivals are now dated by keeping the day date but adding a solar month, so that a celebration once held on the seventh day of the seventh month now occurs on August 7. Finally, and more rarely, a few special days retain their lunar dating completely, so that they rotate backward against the solar year. From the solar point of view, therefore, these are moveable feasts. Since the late nineteenth century the timing of the major festivals has been coordinated so that all the larger shrines observe them at the same time. But there are still many distinctive local and regional festivities attached to individual shrines, such as the rituals dedicated to the patron deities of particular places. In addition to the liturgical calendar, an important related feature is the Japanese custom of dividing history according to imperial reigns or epochs. Emperor Hirohito died in 1989, ending the Showa era, and his son Akihito's accession inaugurated the Heisei epoch.

30. How important is the *concept of "ritual"* in Confucianism and the CIT? Could you describe an example of an annual CIT ritual occasion?

There is perhaps no more fundamental notion in Chinese religious thought generally than that of *li,* proper ritual. The Chinese term is composed of two elements meaning sacrifice and spirit—more precisely, "contact with the upper world" combined with a character that once depicted a sacred vessel. It applies to all religious ceremony, from the most "popular" to the most official imperial cultic worship. Historically under the oversight of a Ministry of Rites, state rituals have generally been the most formal and precise. Pre-modern ritual practice distinguished several levels of ceremony. Supreme Offerings, performed mostly by the emperor himself, addressed Heaven, Earth, the forebears of the emperor and empress, and the deities of earth and seed. Middle Offerings propitiated sun and moon, ancestors of previous reigns, the god of agriculture called Emperor Shen Nung, and the goddess of silk production, Leizu. Lower Offerings occurred in local or regional state temples and revered Guandi as deity of war, Wenzhang as deity of literature, and Sage Emperor Fuxi, among others. When Confucius spoke of *li,* he had in mind all of these, plus the entire range of ceremonies enacted on a smaller scale or in private. But more than that, he conceived of *li* as informing all proper human relationships.

At the Temple of Heaven in Beijing, a major event occurred at the winter solstice. Preparations commenced two months in advance. With five days to go, authorities inspected the animals to be offered. The next day they prepared the hall in which the emperor would spend a day in spiritual preparation, and the day after that the emperor began his abstinence. A procession made its way from the Forbidden City to the Temple, with common folk taking care not to look at the royal person as he passed by. The emperor spent that day and night in the so-called Hall of Abstinence, a large complex to the west of the main north-south axis and about halfway between the Altar of Heaven to the south and the Hall of Harvest Prayer at the north of the compound. He bathed ritually and fasted for a day. (Later emperors often prepared in the Forbidden City itself.) Two days before the solstice, ritualists made final preparation of all ceremonial objects for the emperor's review. The day before the solstice, the emperor left the Hall of Abstinence and proceeded to the Altar of Heaven to honor Shangdi and his own royal forbears with incense and bowing, and then returned to the Hall of Abstinence. Early the next day, he began a nine-part ceremony. At the round Altar of Heaven, where his ancestors' spirit tablets were arrayed, animals were sacrificed and he paid obeisance to the ancestors. Offerings included silk and jade as well as the sacrificial meats. To music and dancing, he presented wine to Shangdi and the spirits in the first of three such offerings. After the emperor bade the sacred presences farewell he withdrew to an observation dais, while officials consigned the offerings to a furnace. The ceremonies ended with the emperor exiting by the south gate and returning to the Forbidden City.

31. What *regular* or *annual observances* have been part of *Confucian/CIT* tradition?

For many centuries Confucians celebrated in their temples with large feasts in the Master's honor at both the vernal and autumnal equinoxes, corresponding with the second and eighth lunar months. During the fourth of the night's five watches, celebrants paid homage to Confucius's ancestors and then moved to the central memorial hall at sunrise. Arrayed carefully across the entire main courtyard were row on row of participants according to rank, with imperial bureaucrats along the sides and six groupings of students in the center. Before and within the memorial hall the offerings and sacrificial animals were arranged. These included a roll of silk, vessels full of wine, soup, and various foods, and a ritually slaughtered ox flanked by a pig and a lamb. A lengthy order of ceremony included specific offerings of each of the items, to Confucius and then to the other sages enshrined in the main hall, along with profound bowing and prostration, and songs of praise. All was accompanied by full classical Chinese orchestra and punctuated by booming drum beats to mark changes in the action. In addition to those semi-annual festivities, smaller semi-monthly observances included offerings to the spirit of Confucius at each new and full moon. In Korea, at the spring and autumn equinoxes, Confucians honor both Korean and Chinese sages at the Confucian University's shrine.

Each year on the day before the winter solstice, the emperor and his retinue visited the Temple of Heaven for an elaborate event. When paying homage to Heaven and Earth, the emperor would perform special gestures of humility by kneeling three times and prostrating himself nine times. When he sacrificed to other powers, such as the sun, the moon, and the gods with power over the forces of nature, the emperor did not perform these rituals of self-abasement. At the Forbidden City's Hall of Supreme Harmony, major sacred events included the enthronement of a new emperor, royal weddings, an event every ten years called the Great Anniversary, the announcement of results of civil service examinations, and celebrations of the winter solstice and new year. In the Hall of Middle Harmony, the emperor formulated decrees to be made public in royal temples at all the various seasonal festivities. Imperial officials designated by the emperor, or local administrators in the case of smaller events, took care of the regular agriculturally significant occasions throughout the country.

Many of the religiously significant times acknowledged with rituals in sacred sites affiliated with the CIT overlap with popular Daoist and CCT practices. The Literati, who functioned as ritual specialists in service of the imperial house, generally looked down on Daoist and CCT devotionalism and often made fun of their beliefs. But as servants of the emperor, they could hardly afford to snub the very deities to whom the general populace prayed for success in mundane but necessary concerns such as timely rain and an abundant harvest. When the emperor's political administrators dispatched across the land entered into their roles as religious ritualists, they often found themselves crossing an imaginary line from the elite to the everyday life of local folk. Celebrating days associated with deities of purely local or regional origin and importance remained the task of Daoists and practitioners of CCT. But when they paid homage to local or regional deities whom the emperor had elevated to the CIT pantheon, the Literati were providing implicit legitimation for popular beliefs and practices. In addition to the Birthday of Confucius on the twenty-seventh day of the eighth lunar month, the CIT also celebrated new and full moon occasions, some of which coincided with feasts like that of Laozi (second month, fifteenth day) and the Hungry Ghosts (seventh month, fifteenth day).

32. What are the major types of *Daoist religious observance?*

Daoist sources talk about three levels of ceremony. "Great Services" called *jiao,* which occur relatively infrequently; "Ritual Gatherings" called *fanhui;* and "Feast Days" called *tan.* Two essential features of every religious celebration are the preparation and the actual event. *Zhai* refers to several types of purifying fast. Strictly speaking the *zhai* is preparatory to the main ceremonial feature, the offering or *jiao,* but certain distinct actions set the purification apart. Both celebrants and their sacred space need to be prepared ritually. To purify both mind and body, participants meditate in solitude, eat vegetarian meals, fast for a time, and refrain from sex. Preparation may commence as much as three days ahead, for the major feasts, and continues through the main event itself. Celebrants prepare the sacred space through a combination of actions including chanting and burning incense. The category of events called *jiao* includes various kinds of festivities. In ancient times the principal *jiao* were associated with planting and harvest. Eventually various Daoist sects incorporated elements of the time-honored traditions into their liturgies but the agricultural element became secondary. Different groups compiled extensive collections of liturgical rites in massive tomes, with ceremonies designed for a wide range of occasions.

For virtually every temple community, the principal deity's birthday provides the occasion for a major yearly festivity. Celebrants focus on the temple and the main icon, sprucing up and getting the deity decked out in new finery. In addition there are dozens of other special days, some of which are the following. New Year emphasizes a fresh start, with Laozi's feast on the first day and special prayers to the Jade Pure One on the eighth and the Jade Emperor on the ninth day of the first month. The latter is a lengthy festivity that culminates on the fifteenth with the Lantern Festival. "Clear and Bright" happens on the first day of the third month. (In mainland China this is not lunar but occurs always on April 5.) Its main thrust is to remember the dead, maintain burial places, and offer ritual meals at the graves.

Dragon Boat races on the fifth day of the fifth month commemorate the drowning of a poet of old. More important, however, is the association of that month with the need to ward off spirits of disease at a time when, with the summer solstice approaching, Yin energy begins to replace Yang as the dominant energy. CCT devotees celebrate Guan Yin's ascension to heaven on the nineteenth of the sixth month, during which people also mark the mid-point in the year. On the seventh day of the seventh month, people observe the one night when the Weaving Maid and the Cowherd, a celestial couple, can be together. And the fifteenth marks the birthday of a Daoist deity called the Earth Controller, known in CCT as the emperor-sage Shun.

Numerous rituals acknowledging the need to placate the wandering dead occupy many during the seventh month. Most prominent is the Ghost Festival on the fifteenth day, when people seek to propitiate the spirits by leaving food out for them. Although it was formerly a Buddhist observance, Daoist masters now officiate at the occasion. A mid-autumn celebration of the moon goddess's birthday, once a harvest festival, occurs on the fifteenth of the eighth month. On the ninth day of the ninth month, called Double-

Yang because of the auspicious nature of the number nine, people once sought protection in amulets and fled lowland evil by taking to the hills. Nowadays, most folks simply go for walks in the cool fresh autumn air. On the fifteenth of the tenth month, worshipers mark the birthday of a Daoist deity called the Controller of the Waters known in CCT as the sage Yu. A winter festivity marks the solstice during the eleventh month. Before the twelfth month is even half spent, planning begins for the New Year.

One Daoist/CCT observance outdoes the rest in scale. A grand affair called the ritual of Cosmic Renewal occurs at varying intervals in different places. It was once on a sixty-year cycle, according to the ancient calendar reckoning calculated with the "branches and stems." Some temples celebrate this way as often as every ten years now. Whenever a community erects a new temple it is time for a renewal ritual. This major festival belongs to the larger category called *jiao.* Ritual specialists from the so-called Black Hat group have exclusive rights to officiate at these events. A standard feature is recitation from the *Jade Emperor Scripture,* and the focus of prayer is on seeking blessings of all kinds for the future. Massive organizational efforts precede the larger celebrations. Interviews are conducted with prospective high priests from among whom the committee can choose a leader who will then arrange for a full staff of ritual specialists. Full-scale festivities require extensive construction of temporary altars or shrines. Celebrations nowadays typically go on for from three to five days, though they formerly lasted as long as nearly two months.

Other important Daoist/CCT celebrations include the following: Daoists observe days devoted to the Three Officials (or Officers or Rulers), whom CCT name Shun, Yao, and Yu, on the fifteenth days of the first, seventh, and tenth lunar months. Their days are associated respectively with heaven, earth, and water. The Heavenly Official, Shun, ranks highest and remains very popular in Taiwan, for example. The Water Official, Yu, is celebrated for having saved the world from uncontrolled flooding. Three Daoist deities considered to be at the pinnacle of the pantheon are known as the Three Primordials. Their festival days coincide with those of the Three Officials, respectively, the first two of which also coincide with the CCT Lantern Festival and Ghost Festival.

33. What are some of the major *festivities Shinto* practitioners celebrate?

"Five seasonal days" *(gosekku)* celebrate simple but essential blessings. Timing of the five seasonal days is still based on the lunar calendar, but transferred to the solar months. For example, the days were originally observed on the third day of the third lunar month, the fifth of the fifth, the seventh of the seventh, and the ninth of the ninth. The days now retain the same position, but in solar months of the same numbers. Seven Herbs Day now falls on January 7, when people greet the springtime with a specially seasoned soup. For *Hinamatsuri,* or Doll Festival (nowadays called Girls' Day) on March 3, many people reenact the ancient practice of floating clay or paper dolls on river or sea to ensure the health of their daughters. Boys' Day *(kodomo-no-hi)* falls on May 5, when little boys receive dolls of heroic figures who model valor and loyalty. On July 7, Tanabata or "Seventh Night" recalls the Chinese story of the celestial cowboy and the weaver maid, condemned to be distant stars forever because their romance caused them to slacken their labors. On this night the two reunite briefly on the bridge of the Milky Way. Farmers and textile workers take the opportunity to pray for success in their occupations. Finally, Chrysanthemum Day (Kiku no sekku) falls on the ninth of September. Many still go to local shrines to appreciate the beautifully cultivated flower, which became the official symbol of the emperor during the Meiji era in the mid-nineteenth century.

Many festivities are still tied to various agricultural occasions. Spring and autumn festivals correspond with planting and harvesting. A large cluster of so-called "spring festivals" *(haru-matsuri)* covers events that run generally from January to May, though some areas stretch the season into July. In late March or April people celebrate Cherry Blossom Festival, one of nature's sublime but fleeting glories. On May 5 (fifth day of the fifth month in some places, other days elsewhere) many people observe a special Rice Planting day. Two of Kyoto's larger shrines, Kamigamo and Shimogamo in the north of the city, celebrate a prayer for good harvest called Hollyhock Festival (aoi-matsuri), complete with elaborate processions and reenactments of ancient imperial events. With countless regional variations, the planting (or transplanting) rites occur generally during May, June, and July, stretching well into the summer season. This seasonal overlap is a result of using more than one system for converting special occasions from the lunar to the solar calendar.

Some shrines host enormous gatherings centered around processions and contests of various kinds. Autumn festivals *(aki-matsuri)* include a similar grouping of celebrations that actually begin before the summer festival season has ended and extend into October. At the beginning of each imperial era, the new emperor performs an autumn celebration called the "Great Feast of New Food" *(daijosai),* offering rice to the Sun Goddess and imperial forbears. Whether in the imperial palace or at local shrines, these are all occasions for gratitude to the *kami* for bountiful harvest. Between planting and harvest come a host of generally smaller summer festivals *(natsumatsuri)* during which people pray for a healthy crop. Some shrines, however, still host major celebrations during July, August, and September. Many of these are occasions for younger men and boys especially to engage in spirited competition, teams vying to get their *mikoshi* (processional miniature shrines) along the procession route faster and arrive at the shrine first. Winter festivals *(fuyu no matsuri)* revolve largely around preparations for the end of the year and New Year's celebrations *(shogatsu).* Calculated on the solar calendar, the winter solstice heralds the new year, so many people begin then with ceremonial cleaning and wrap up the old year by laying old sewing needles to rest at a local shrine. Honor for all things that contribute to human civilization—not for human beings alone—that have come to the end of their lives is essential. Seven days during a period called the "great cold" (*daikan,* generally between January sixth and twenty-first) retain some of their ancient associations. People gather at shrines to enjoy the return of the sun in lengthening days that portend spring, and to pray for good fortune in general.

O-Bon Matsuri is one of those feasts whose timing is determined by adding a solar month to the lunar reckoning. Hence, a feast formerly celebrated during the middle (i.e., full moon) of the seventh month now occurs during the middle of the eighth, August. On November 23 and 24 falls the "New Food Festival" *(Niinamesai).* Acting as high priest, the emperor himself leads the ceremonies. When a newly enthroned emperor presides, the feast is called "Great Food Festival" *(daijosai),* and the ritual seals and formalizes the new ruler's accession. This is one of some thirty regular imperial ceremonies *(koshitsu saishi)* that occur through the year, most conducted privately within the palace. The autumnal equinox still calls for quite elaborate observances in some places. Suwa shrine in Nagasaki, for example, holds its annual Okunchi for three full rousing days and nights. Involving a full range of activities from raucous processions to solemn pre-dawn purifications conducted in almost total silence, the festival engages large numbers of worshipers actively. Festivities begin and end with more private rituals designed to bring the *kami* into the ceremony and see them back to their places of repose. Some ceremonies occur often but on a more ad hoc basis than the regularly scheduled festivals. Nearly every new architectural venture occasions religiously inspired observances.

34. What place does *purification* occupy in Shinto ritual? And what are the main features of major *shrine rituals?*

Few traditions place greater emphasis on the need to purify both participants in ceremonies and the place designated for the rites. Just as the primordial deity, Izanagi, purified himself upon exiting from the underworld, so must all worshipers before engaging in sacred rituals. The contrasting states of pollution or spiritual alienation *(kegare)* and ritual-moral purity *(harae)* encompass a great deal of what Shinto tradition considers important. Simple purification with water is a prerequisite to even the simplest acts of worship. As an ordinary part of rituals performed by priests and shrine staff, purification requires waving a special wand over the individuals or their offerings, and sometimes involves sprinkling salt water or salt. Watch a Sumo wrestling match and you will see the behemoth contestants liberally scattering fistfuls of salt across the ring as they enter to confront each other—a clue to the ancient religious associations of the sport.

More elaborate purification involves ceremonial bathing to cleanse the individual of pollution and sin. Priests sometimes purify by immersion before major rites. Some adepts seek out sacred mountain waterfalls and stand beneath their frigid cataracts in winter as an especially potent form of purification. Most important is the ceremony called "great purification," in which priests of the imperial household as well as throughout the country symbolically purify the whole nation—the whole world, according to some interpretations. Reciting special prayers, they mark the middle and end of the year with cleansing. Before a given shrine's major festivals, shrine priests put considerable time and effort into preparation of themselves and of the site. Officiants enter seclusion the day before the festival, bathe several times, and follow strict rules with respect to clothing, food, and abstinence from sexual activity.

Larger rituals typically include four features. Before beginning any sacred act, including the simplest ones, celebrants purify themselves with water or salt. Welcoming the *kami (kamimukae)* is among the first acts of the presiding priest. The invocation is necessary because many *matsuri* begin away from the shrine in places where the *kami* does not ordinarily reside. Then comes the offering to the *kami* (including ancestors, as in Chinese traditions).

A senior priest serves his fellow priests a symbolic communion sip of sake at the conclusion of a new moon ceremony at Itsukushima Jinja, a major shrine on the island of Miyajima, near Hiroshima. He kneels before each in turn until all have been served, then they file out and return to the priests' quarters. Each priest holds a symbol of ancient courtly authority called the *shaku.*

In addition to responding to the obvious requirement of funds to maintain the thousands of shrines great and small all over the country, people make symbolic offerings and the priests in turn formally present them to the deities. Flowers, food and drink, beautiful textiles or jewelry, and even the performance of traditional art forms or sport can be included among offerings.

Entertainment arranged in connection with a religious festival is known as "divine amusement" *(kannigiwai).* When the priestly staff perform elaborate offerings, the chief priest opens the doors of the innermost sanctuary. The priests pass the offerings among themselves and finally the assistant chief priest places the offerings before the sanctuary doors. Ritual specialists then recite prayers, many of ancient origin and some more recently composed, of praise, thanksgiving, historical recollection about the meaning of the particular occasion, all concluded with appropriately humble leave-taking of the *kami* with a gesture called "Sending the *kami* away" *(kamiokuri).* Ceremonies conclude with a kind of communion rite in which the chief priest serves the other members of the ritual staff a symbolic sip of sake. The priests process from the inner worship hall to the outer hall for this rite that is usually brief, depending on the number of officiants participating. Where large crowds are in attendance for some particularly festive occasion, the closing meal can be quite extensive and elaborate, including a share in some of the food just offered to the *kami.* One ritual element notably lacking in Shinto worship is preaching. Since worship is entirely focused on relating ritually to the deities, Shinto tradition does not consider persuasive religious rhetoric a necessary tool.

Four:

AUTHORITY, LAW, AND ETHICS

35. Are there critical concepts about the nature of the *human person?*

Confucianism: Chinese uses the word *xing* to describe "human nature" in its most fundamental form. That term combines the concepts of "life/progeny" with "heart/mind," the two basic constituents of the person. Confucius further described the fully developed person using the term *ren,* a Chinese word that combines the characters for "human being" and "two." A full person, therefore, is one who exists in society, in communication with others. Human beings are always works in progress, ever shaping themselves in pursuit of an elusive goal of perfection. *Ren,* sometimes translated as goodness, human-heartedness, or even love, is that which activates the other four of the so-called "five great virtues"—devotion, justice, wisdom, and propriety. Only in light of *ren* does law function properly, as a guide rather than as a straight-jacket. *Ren's* two components, *jung* (individual) and *shu* (the virtue of reciprocity) allow human beings to enact the principles known as the "mean," the ability to hold feelings in abeyance, and the "measure," by which one can express emotions in balance.

Shinto: Shinto tradition has not given great attention to speculating about the metaphysical aspects of the human person. Conceptions of soul or spirit at the core of human nature tend to be rather fluid, not unlike popular Chinese ideas about these things. Reflecting the various aspects of both human and divine action, soul or spirit *(tama)* can manifest itself as either rich in blessings, granting harmony and union, full of mysterious power, or "rough." Individuals take second place to the needs of society as a whole, and as a result traditional Shinto thought does not reflect in depth about the self apart from the collectivity. Above all, human beings are children of the *kami* and their natural birthright is to benefit from nature's gifts. Society and family, too, as well as nature, are the wellsprings of life. Acknowledging and venerating one's ancestors keeps healthy the link between individual and society because it keeps alive the continuity of heritage.

36. How do Confucians, Daoists, and adherents of Shinto think about the *goal of human life?*

Confucianism: Confucian teaching describes the epitome of the ideal society as the "superior person" *(junzi).* That means an individual who arrives at a high level of personal development through self-discipline and inquiry. The superior person values justice more highly than profit, and prefers to be quiet and serene rather than vulgar and uncongenial. Cultivating a dignified manner, the superior person nevertheless avoids arrogance. Such a person looks first to his or her personal shortcomings rather than blaming others for their lack of understanding or appreciation. It is said that the way of the superior person is a lengthy journey that begins from "right here." Five "constant virtues" characterize the superior person: self-respect, generosity, sincerity, responsibility, and openness to others. Expanding on the earlier teaching of Confucius, Mengzi taught that fully developed human life begins with four things. Compassion leads to true humanity, shame leads to righteousness, reverence and respect to propriety, and a sense of moral value to wisdom. Behind the notion of the superior person lies a deep-seated conviction of human potential for almost unlimited moral growth.

Daoism: Although the principal early sacred texts do not discuss prospects of life after death explicitly, the question of immortality turned into an important issue for Daoists. Archaeological evidence from well over three thousand years ago suggests that many people believed in some sort of survival after death, but that apparently meant a form of extended earthly existence. Religious Daoism does not always make the kind of distinction some traditions make between life here and life hereafter.

Some Daoists have held views not unlike those of many Christians, believing that at death "life is changed, not taken away." But many have argued that if indeed life is a seamless reality, it may be possible to go on indefinitely without crossing that great divide called death. Whatever specific imagery Daoists have used to describe the nature of human life, the underlying point is that the tradition has been keenly interested in promoting a sense of vitality and in helping adherents to develop a positive attitude to the human condition generally.

Shinto: Long-standing Japanese beliefs emphasize the need to engage life here and now with the highest ethical standards. Life on earth is less a preparation for some ultimate reckoning and accountability, than a call to moral uprightness in tune with a natural world whose forces are ultimately more positive than negative. Commitment to affirming life as one finds it constitutes the highest ethical calling.

37. Is there a distinctive *religious* or *theological "ethic"* in these traditions?

Confucianism: A Confucian formulation of the universal Golden Rule at first strikes the ear as rather negative and passive: "Do not do to others what you do not want done to you." But the Confucian ethic turns out to be overwhelmingly active and positive because of its emphasis on cultivating the natural human capacity for virtue. The Master's positive approach revolves around several key concepts. First and foremost is *li,* principle or propriety, consisting of a whole range of directives for human behavior. Much of *li* arises from the customs that embody the spirit of community. When people can rely on propriety in all relationships, as enshrined in time-honored practice, they experience assurance and freedom in their relationships. Confucius gathered a huge catalogue of social rituals, not out of antiquarian curiosity, but as a way of preserving what he considered the best of tradition. Ritual propriety is meant not to confine but to give a sense of lightness and freedom. Without *li,* he thought, there can be no justice, no morality, for a society without propriety has no foundation in respect. Of equal importance is the notion of *shu,* reciprocity in interpersonal relationships. Reciprocity is essential to putting *li* into action, for it governs the five principal human relationships and the ten associated virtues. In the father-son relationship, the father must cultivate kindness, the son reverence. The elder brother must deal gently with the younger brother, who responds with respect. A mutuality of faithfulness and obedience should characterize husband-wife relationships. Let all elders be considerate of those younger, and expect deference in return. Finally, a ruler must strive to treat subjects with benevolence and benefit from their loyalty as a result.

Daoism: Daoism's version of the Golden Rule is this: If a person treats me well, I do so in return. If that person treats me unjustly, I nevertheless respond with goodness, like the ever-constant Dao. The central ethical principle is the enigmatic concept of *wu wei.* The term translates literally as "non-action" or "non-effort," but it means something like "acting naturally." *Wu wei* is the ultimate in "natural law." All things behave according to their inherent makeup. Human beings alone have a tendency to get it wrong by trying to take control where we have no business doing so—and where there is ultimately no good reason for doing so. Only by observing the Way of nature can people hope to grasp this elusive principle of uncontrived accomplishment. *Wu wei* is not to be confused with laziness or indifference. Observe how nature brings about whatever is needed without stratagem or artifice. Nature does act, of course, and there is no lack of struggle in its doings, but it always returns to equilibrium. The key, then, is acting spontaneously, but that is not a recommendation for acting impulsively. Behind the Daoist principle is the conviction that human beings will act for the greater good so long as they are not merely reacting to unreasonable social or governmental restraints. Genuine moral leadership requires authentic altruism, the desire to lead by serving—the diametric opposite of demagoguery. Concern for effective government in a time of social and institutional disintegration seems to have given rise to the notion of *wu wei.* But Daoism's sages embodied the principle in a way that recommended it as a fundamental religious and philosophical value.

Shinto: Some have characterized Shinto as a type of naturalistic humanism that begins with the conviction of innate human goodness. When evil gains the ascendancy, it is not because of some inherent or inherited human tendency. Evil advances whenever human beings lose concentration on life at its simplest, most basic level. As an ethical ideal, the concept of *makoto* means something like genuineness or authenticity. An ethical person is one who characteristically makes choices unspoiled by ulterior motives. Purity of intention thus takes precedence over adherence to any specific set of commands and prohibitions. Scholars refer to an ethic of this kind as "contextual" or "situational." All acts derive their moral value from the overall setting in which people perform them. A virtuous person is one who enjoys maximum harmony with the totality of the powers of nature. How does one assess the quality of virtue? The ethical barometer is a faculty called *kokoro,* a term that suggests a union of mind and heart. What some traditions call purity of heart, Shinto tradition calls brightness *(seimei).* Purified of all ill intent, the mind and heart are illumined through intimacy with the divine. Individuals do not evaluate their actions in terms of whether they will reap reward or suffer punishment as a consequence. They think rather of how their actions might affect the life of the community here and now. How does one know when he or she has crossed the moral divide? Shame is a very powerful index of morality in Shinto tradition. What members of some traditions identify as moral guilt incurred objectively as a result of some specific act, Shinto tradition regards as a breach of social contract for which the individual ought to be ashamed and seek forgiveness through purification.

38. What is the principal _Confucian virtue?_ What is meant by _"rectification of names"?_

Behind all the other virtues, what makes a good Confucian is "filial devotion" or _xiao._ The Chinese term is composed of "son" with "old" placed above it. Confucius taught that all moral virtue, and indeed civilization itself, flows from filial devotion. As a bare minimum, one should do no harm to one's parents. Filial devotion culminates in doing one's family proud. Traditional texts go into great detail about how one ought to treat parents, summarizing ideal behavior in five duties: reverence always, joyful service, solicitude for ailing parents, sincere grief at a parent's death, and proper ritual veneration thereafter. Lack of filial devotion in Confucius's time was a most serious offense. Individuals could be put to death for cursing their elders. Filial devotion was the very bedrock of social order, a fundamental acknowledgment of authority on the family level without which there could be no exercise of authority in society at large. Chinese tradition regards society as built on the family. Sons and daughters do not "go out" into the world as they reach maturity. Rather than "leaving the nest," they invest themselves in the family, knowing that their children will do the same. Only in that way can the foundations of society as a whole remain firm.

"Rectification of names" was a principle in Confucius's quest for moral renewal. If Confucius were here today he would surely be aghast at the way inflated language seems to have taken over ordinary conversation. "I was so tired I was _literally_ dead on my feet." No you weren't, he might say. Drop the "literally" and your expression will have far more impact, even though your surrounding culture insists that more is better. He would be amazed to hear restaurant staff introduce themselves as "your food and beverage counselor" or hear store cashiers and stockers identified as "sales associates" and "inventory specialists." But Confucius would worry less about such trivial items than about the very same deep social issues he agonized over in his own time. When a man fails to show respect to his parents, do not call him a son. If he fails to guide his children, he is unworthy to be called a father. If a woman does not attend to her family faithfully, one can hardly call her a wife or mother. If a man is unfaithful to his wife, do not call him a husband. Of greatest political import is his insistence that no unjust ruler deserves the name "emperor." Beneath this apparently nit-picking criticism, Confucius was getting at a profound truth: over the long haul, imprecise speech allows injustice to go unnoticed because it can hide behind acceptable names. Euphemism can erode one's sense of right and wrong and desensitize a person to violence. In other words, it is easier to get away with a misdeed ethically if conventional speech appears to discount it linguistically. Eventually we persuade ourselves that "mis-speaking" is not a lie, that stealing is merely the redistribution of wealth. In the long run, Confucius believed, language matters because it not only reflects, but can even change, the way we think.

39. What is the basic Confucian concept of appropriate *moral leadership?* And what is the *Mandate of Heaven?*

Confucius believed that order was essential for bringing out the best in human beings. He and his disciples rejected the early Daoist notion that all things work for the best if only people learn the ways of nature and that there is no need for government or military force or oppressive laws. In Confucius's view government was essential, and that almost always meant bureaucratic structures. But he believed the external trappings had to be supported by a foundation of example rather than coercion. No one can bring about the good society by force of will. One can only foster appropriate government by creating an environment of propriety, reciprocity, and good music—yes, good music. Law, he believed, can erode moral values, because people often prefer to act a certain way merely to escape punishment. The example of a great leader is preferable, for it instills a sense of healthy shame that leads people to seek improvement. Confucius was a realist, however, and conceded that law was often a practical necessity.

What he wanted for the people most of all was the sense of confidence that can grow when people feel prosperous and educated. A good leader knows how to bring out the best in his people and how to wield authority deftly. But as a concession to the vast differences among human beings, government needs levels of power—some can lead, some can support a leader, some can follow but may not understand why they ought to do so. A leader knows how to cultivate conditions conducive to the betterment of society by tapping the roots of human resources rather than waiting until the plant is fully grown and incapable of nurturance.

Confucians have interpreted the concept of Mandate or Will of Heaven in various ways over the centuries. As an ingredient in Confucian political thought, the concept has functioned both as a means of legitimation of the regime in power and a justification for overthrowing a corrupt regime. The notion ultimately derives from a traditional Chinese belief in an elaborate network of correspondences between all levels of existence, the heavenly, the earthly, and the human. Human beings are not the independent source of authority. They can hope for harmony only through sensitivity to the ways of Heaven above and of nature below. Order in society depends on the good-faith effort of a single human being, the emperor as "Son of Heaven," to rule unselfishly by consulting incessantly the Will of Heaven. A theory of immanent retribution holds that there is a direct connection between natural and moral evil in the world and Heaven's displeasure with any emperor who arrogantly forgets the source of his authority. When the people prosper, one can conclude with certainty that affairs of state are in order, all as a direct result of the emperor's keeping his priorities straight. Many of the great Confucian thinkers have taught that the tradition's consistent contribution has been that of fearlessly holding the ruler responsible to his people. If the one on the throne presides over an unjust regime, that person is no longer worthy of the name "emperor." According to Mengzi, for example, the people have the right to remove such a fraudulent leader. Mengzi argued that violent overthrow of an unjust ruler was not regicide but tyrannicide. The greatest sovereign, therefore, is the one who governs only after first submitting to a higher authority.

40. Is there a *central teaching authority* in any of the major Chinese and Japanese traditions?

Confucianism/CIT: One could argue that the social institution of the Literati functioned as a central teaching authority. There is no doubt that they set up the system to which any person of talent and ambition who wished to advance would have to conform. Complete with its regimen of demanding examinations, degrees, and apprenticeships, the Literati system of public service also had its religious implications, given the overall context in which traditional Chinese saw the role of the emperor. And there is no doubt that the system offered little or no flexibility—make the grade or wash out. The Literati system was, therefore, a central teaching authority at least for a limited segment of society. Even the ordinary folk in towns and villages came under the indirect influence of the system. But the system did not make its demands on the "average" person the way it did on those who aspired to rise within its ranks.

Daoism/CCT: Individual Daoist sects, orders, and schools have, and in some cases still do, regarded their teaching office as a solemn and demanding role. But, on the whole, Daoists do not think of themselves as following any particular teaching or adhering to a particular orthodoxy. Even when important patriarchs, such as the living leader of the Celestial Masters school, have delivered formal pronouncements, relatively few Daoists take notice. What is true of Daoism in this respect is even truer of the much more amorphous CCT. In neither case is any specific articulation of doctrine of any particular importance. Doctrinal standards are replaced here by pure tradition—"the way we've always done things."

Shinto: Shinto's close identification over the centuries with Japanese culture and imperial rule has sometimes made it appear that the royal administration functioned as a central religious authority. Certain regimes have made concerted efforts to encourage uniformity of traditional thinking among the Japanese people, and that has sometimes involved "official" statements about Shinto beliefs as well as attempts to centralize the organization of large numbers of shrines. In addition, training for Shinto ritual specialists has in recent times devolved on only a select few educational institutions very much associated with "national" identity. Those academic-religious organizations have set themselves the task of clarifying and, in some cases, restructuring the countless elements of ancient Shinto tradition into a coherent system. Theirs has been an increasingly theological enterprise in modern times. Even so, Shinto tradition has remained quite fluid and inclusive, and far less identified with the definitive teaching authority than, say, Roman Catholicism. Over the centuries, various centralized institutions have come and gone. The Institute of the Great Teaching *(daikyoin),* for example, was motivated largely by the desire to root out Buddhist and Christian influences in nineteenth-century Japan. The Bureau of Divinity *(jingikan)* sought to unify the administration of shrines and the appointment of priests. It is perhaps best to think of the centralized authority as regulating matters of practice rather than of belief, setting out detailed instructions for rituals *(jinja shaishiki),* and for coordinating observances nationally.

41. Have the Chinese and Japanese evolved discrete *systems of religious law?*

Confucianism/CIT: The Confucian tradition's closest analogy to the kind of religious regulation of importance to Jews and Muslims, for example, is the canons of ritual. It may sound at first as though Confucian law is limited to what are sometimes called "rubrics." (Rubrics are instructions on how to perform a ceremony; they take their name from the Latin for "red" because the directions are printed in red ink to set them off from the liturgical

text.) But what Confuci
includes an enormous r
cian scholars have codi
tion in life, from mem
servant who prepares fr
self. These often elabora
tions might strike the
compulsive. But the trad
cultivated virtue will alw
cisely his or her relations
ing. In this way, Confuci
hierarchy still very much

Shinto: There hav
concerning the structu
system, and about
gious organizati
tionships be
and Budd
liberty
fic

of Korea and Japan, as well as of China. Because of its unique relationship to the civil authority represented by the emperor, Confucianism as such, with its Five Classics and Four Books, did not develop a specific code of penal law. That was still largely the province of the Literati as royal administrators, but it emanated from the imperial household and developed over many centuries.

Daoism: Apart from the charters or disciplinary codes of Daoist organizations such as monastic orders, there is no such thing as formal Daoist religious law. The very idea goes against the grain of the concept of natural balance and harmony that is so central to Daoist thought. That is not to say that there aren't countless standard practices and expectations as to behavior. The difference between Daoism and, say, Islam or Christianity, in this respect is that the Muslim and Christian traditions have systematically codified those expectations while the Daoist tradition has not. Every cultural and religious system has its standards and sanctions. But in the cases of both Islam and Christianity, independent legal systems became necessary largely because the religious traditions expanded into new cultural settings very different from those in which the traditions arose. In the case of Daoism, religion and culture have been much more closely and consistently identified, making a separate system of religious law largely unnecessary.

been numerous bodies of legislation
re and administration of the Shinto shrine
overnmental controls over the spread of reli-
ons in Japan generally. Laws have decreed rela-
ween imperial rule and religion, and between Shinto
ism, and others have stipulated conditions for religious
But there has never been the kind of comprehensive codi-
tion of religious law that one finds, for example, in Islam's
Shari'a, Judaism's rabbinical law, or Roman Catholicism's canon
law. Virtually everything related to the regulation of conduct in
Shinto tradition has been integrated into an all-encompassing and
very demanding, but mostly unwritten, code of ethics. People
learn what is expected of them religiously through family and
local community tradition.

42. Are there important *hierarchical structures* in these religious traditions?

Confucianism/CIT: Confucian thought discerns an essential need for hierarchies in all aspects of human society. It is a
question of order. Human beings may be identical in essence, but
they clearly differ in personal attributes, talents, knowledge, and
age, to name only a few distinguishing characteristics. Confucius
believed that realism required recognition of those differences.
Take the challenge of living an ethical life, for example. Each
stage in life has its unique problems. Young people need to con-
quer sensuality, adults combativeness, and the elderly greed. As
for the variety of human capabilities, Confucius saw four levels:
those who possess knowledge from birth, those capable of
becoming "superior persons" by acquiring knowledge, those who
learn only with great effort, and those not at all disposed to learning. Confucian thinking has often been very class-conscious. The
Master believed that society needed stratification in order to function smoothly. At the top was the scholar, supported by the farmer
who produced life's basic needs, artisans who make practical

items from what farmers grow, merchants who buy and sell what others produce, and soldiers who, unfortunately, often wreck what others make.

Within the highest echelons of the Confucian hierarchy there were still further distinctions. Until around 1530, those enshrined in Confucian memorial halls were ranked with titles taken from imperial administration. Confucian greats were honored as king, duke, marquis, or earl, for example. After 1530, Confucians replaced those royal honorifics with the titles sage, correlate, especially learned one, worthy one, and scholar. Over the course of history, some individuals within the Confucian hierarchy have been promoted in rank, others have been demoted, and still others have been restored after having been demoted. Such hierarchical adjustments have depended a great deal on ideological leanings within various imperial regimes, with the last major rearrangement occurring around 1724. The CIT was, of course, hierarchical, but with the emperor at the top and a much higher position for the military.

Daoism: Since there are many different sects and schools, there are no official and universally acknowledged hierarchical structures that unite all Daoists. But there are de facto hierarchies, both religious (within individual Daoist organizations) and social (based on a broader kind of class-consciousness). For example, in the Celestial Masters school, the living Heavenly Master functioned as a sort of archbishop, overseeing the running of the school's temples in the region. Within the administration of the school, ranks were named after those of the imperial bureaucracy, such as libationer, recorder, and director of ceremonies. The Celestial Masters school has retained much of its ancient hierarchical structure today. In addition, each of the various monastic orders is internally structured according to authority and leadership roles, with the equivalent of an abbot at the head. Hierarchical structures have also been very much a part of the several short-lived attempts to create theocratic states, but their claims to authority were naturally limited. Within their everyday lives, most Daoists would likely be aware only of the functional hierarchy inherent in the more elaborate ritual celebrations. There a high priest presides, while subordinate priests perform much of the ceremonial action and musical accompaniment. Other non-ordained assistants busy themselves with the overall mechanics of the ritual, keeping the action moving by making sure necessary supplies are plentiful and other practical matters are in order.

Shinto: Like so many other religious traditions, Shinto community structures often reflect the belief that human life mirrors divine life. Just as there is at least an implicit hierarchy among divine beings, human society needs a certain degree of structure. Long-standing Japanese tradition, much influenced and reinforced by Confucian teaching over the centuries, lays great emphasis on knowing one's place in society. Each individual stands in a relationship of higher-to-lower, or vice-versa, with his or her fellow human beings, and basic etiquette requires that one be aware of social subordination in every context.

Everyday Japanese speech, with its various levels of polite address, reflects that awareness. Though contemporary Japan is a democratic society, with all the political institutions needed to support a democracy, a sense of hierarchy runs deep in the culture and so in Shinto belief and practice. Everything from ranks within the network of shrines to division of labor among ritual specialists mirrors that awareness of multi-level structure in society at large. For several centuries in the early history of Shinto, four groups were responsible for most Shinto ritual. The Nakatomi family oversaw ritual generally, the Imbe family were concerned with maintaining ritual purity, the Urabe family focused on divinatory rituals so as to know the divine intentions in all matters, and shrine musicians performed the "divine entertainments." Other powerful clans or families held and relinquished positions of power and influence over subsequent centuries.

43. How does the *hierarchy among Shinto shrines* work?

Over the centuries Shinto authorities have devised a number of structures and classifications by which to distinguish various levels and functions of shrines. The most important is called the "shrine-rank system" *(shakaku seido)* that has been in place since shortly after the Meiji restoration of 1868. The term *jingu* designates shrines of top rank under imperial auspices, such as Meiji Jingu, in Tokyo, which enshrines royal ancestors, and Ise Jingu, which is at the top of the hierarchy and is called the *Daijingu,* Grand Imperial Shrine. Next in rank are the approximately one hundred thousand *jinja,* a generic term including virtually all shrines larger than little wayside structures. About two hundred and fifty are included on a special list of highest ranking shrines. Of these, some two hundred were designated prior to World War II as "governmental shrines" *(kansha).*

Many larger *jinja* have spawned affiliated or branch shrines called *bunsha.* Multiple shrines dedicated to a single *kami* generally constitute distinct families, with one shrine usually acknowledged as the original foundation from which branch shrines developed. Some very important *jinja,* such as Kasuga in Nara and about a dozen others, have the honorific title *taisha,* "grand shrine," roughly equivalent to "cathedral basilica." They are also part of a cluster of twenty-two institutions *(nijuni sha)* elevated to special status, but even they are divided into three levels, seven highest, seven middle ranking, and eight lower. That grouping arose out of the practice of ranking shrines within a given region according to their order of priority on pilgrimage routes or to guide devotees intent on visiting a sequence of holy places.

In various prefectures, a further ranking of area shrines simply lists them as "first, second, or third" shrine, acknowledging the three regional shrines that draw the largest crowds of worshipers. A number of *jinja* (some count a hundred and thirty-eight) have been specially designated as "nation-protecting shrines" *(gokoku jinja)* because of their dedication to the souls of those who died in battle. Twenty-seven shrines within that category, also called "deceased spirit-invoking shrines" *(shokonsha),* have been accorded a special rank because of the importance of the heroes from all periods of Japanese history that they commemorate. Tokyo's Yasukuni Jinja ranks at the top of that category. Prior to 1945, countless smaller local memorials represented the bottom of this hierarchical category. The main central administration is called the Association of Shinto Shrines (Jinja Honcho), which has branches (called *jinja cho)* in each Japanese prefecture.

44. What are some of the main varieties of *officials* or *ritual specialists?*

Confucianism/CIT: Strictly speaking, Confucians have no separate structure of ritual officials. Bureaucrats of the imperial administration were responsible for offerings performed in Confucian memorial halls. The emperor himself was the supreme ritual specialist in the sense that he exercised sole rights to perform certain ceremonies judged essential to the good order of life under Heaven. All subordinate, regional, and local ceremonies were delegated to the various ranks of the Literati. Today, even in the absence of imperial structures, government officials still play such roles. In imperial times, the emperor's administration was divided into nine departments. Most important in this context was the Imperial Academy, whose chief officer was the Minister of Ceremonies. His function was similar to that of chief priest, since he was responsible for rituals performed in all imperial temples. A common ritual at local imperial altars required that a newly appointed local magistrate stay overnight before his official installation in the temple of the "spirit magistrate," a deity who was the earthly magistrate's celestial counterpart.

Daoism: Since about the fourth century C.E., religious specialists called *daoshi,* "masters of the Dao," have led Daoist communities at prayer. These leaders can be celibate monks (there are also nuns called *daogu*) who live almost exclusively in monastic communities. Monastic priests—mostly members of the Perfect

Realization order—occasionally perform public rituals, but, not unlike cloistered monks in some other traditions, their principal focus is on their more private spiritual pursuits. Some ritual specialists are married family men who live near a monastery. These so-called "lay masters" *(shigong)* make up the majority of Daoist ritual specialists. Individuals generally specialize in certain types of ritual, such as exorcism and faith-healing. Among non-monastic types, the ritualists whose functions most closely resemble those of priests in various other traditions are called the Black Hats. Many of them belong to the Celestial Masters school, perhaps the oldest of all Daoist organizations. In addition to the Black Hats, the "official" and intricately trained priests, there are the Red Turbans known as *fashi,* specialists in the occult. Black Hats, so called because of their small mandarin cap with a gold knob on top, are authorized to perform at both the greater festivals and the more ordinary ceremonies to which the Red Turbans are restricted. (The two groups are alternatively known as Blackheads and Redheads.) Specialists of earlier times called "libationers" in the Celestial Masters school had the triple duty of religious instruction, local administration, and ritual leadership, not unlike the typical parish pastor in many Christian denominations.

Shinto: Shinto tradition refers to the priesthood in general as either *shinshoku* or *kannushi*. Larger shrines with full priestly staffs distinguish among a number of ranks. The chief priest is called the *guji,* generally the highest ranking local official. The *guji* might have oversight of up to thirty subordinate shrines. The *gonguji* is second-in-command and oversees a staff of several lower ranks as well, including junior assistant chief priests *(shingonguji).* Senior priests *(negi),* assistant senior priests *(gonnegi),* and regular priests *(shuten* or *kujo)* fill out the ranks of male staff. A national ranking system also distinguishes among priests by acknowledging their levels of learning with the equivalent of academic degrees named "purity" *(jokai),* "brightness" *(meikai),* "righteousness" *(seikai),* and "uprightness" *(chokkai).* Young unmarried women called shrine maidens *(miko)* function rather like deaconesses. Dressed in striking vermilion skirts and white blouses, they assist in blessing rituals, run the shrine shop, and perform sacred dances. *Miko* traditionally begin their association with the shrine and training for service as "sacred children." Highest of all in rank is the unique position called *saishu,* found only at the Ise shrine and held by a woman. She is an imperial princess with the symbolic title "Master of the *Matsuri* (Festivals)." Assisting her is a priest with the rank of *daiguji,* "great chief priest," a function unique to Ise. In the imperial household, ritual specialists have either of two ranks. The *shoten* parallels the shrine rank of senior priest, the *shotenho* that of assistant senior priest. But the emperor himself or a personal delegate presides at over two dozen annual ceremonies, much as the Chinese sovereign once did over CIT rituals.

45. How are leaders *chosen and vested with authority?*

Confucianism/CIT: Priestly orders or classes in many traditions derive their authority from either hereditary lineage or from a perceived ability to manage spiritual power, or both of these. The case of the Literati as a special class is quite different in many respects. Their role in imperial religious affairs may have originated with the office of royal astrologer, a person possessed of arcane knowledge. They had to understand all there was to know about how to plan imperial matters in perfect coordination with the rhythms of the cosmos. But the Literati's continued prestige rested on their identification with a broader range of knowledge, that of literature, history, and writing. Their privileged access to the canonical texts, the Classics and Books of Confucian tradition, gave them unquestioned authority. The Literati oversaw virtually every detail of imperial ritual and administration (so much of which was highly ritualized) and were responsible for propriety and auspiciousness in all affairs of the state under Heaven. They were in effect a kind of lay priesthood whose patron and model was Confucius. Prospective members of the Literati underwent extensive education designed to imbue them with the classical texts, an exquisite sensitivity to the nuances of ritual, and an appreciation of the social and political implications of the relationships implied in the great rituals. Literati achieved their various ranks within the hierarchical structure on the basis of their achievement in the imperial examinations. From about the seventh century C.E. on, an elaborate system of examinations could give access to any of three degrees or ranks, each requiring as many as ten different kinds of examination. The Board of Rites oversaw the examinations and the Board of Civil Office made the final appointments. An important feature of this system was that, at least in theory, it bestowed authority on the basis of personal achievement rather than heredity or social status. The higher the rank of a local government's main official, the greater the prestige of its ancestral temple.

Daoism: Traditional Daoist priesthood has long been a hereditary occupation, though that appears to be changing in recent times. This feature obviously applied consistently only to non-celibate branches of the priesthood. Individuals who have successfully completed requisite initial training are ordained, following general patterns similar to those of Buddhist monastic practice. Ordination requires a quorum of ordained priests, and the ordinand takes "refuge" in the Dao, the canon of scripture, and the tradition's spiritual teachers, much as the Buddhist monk takes refuge in the Buddha, the Dharma, and the Sangha. Lay specialists, whether Black Hats or Red Turbans, apprentice to an authoritative master called a *daojang*—perhaps the equivalent of "high priest." His task is to lead novices through several levels of ritual assistantship. Students begin with basic musical accompaniment, learn to watch over the incense burners, and lead group prayers. More difficult training includes learning to chant and memorizing often intricate rubrics (ritual movements). After learning to copy sacred texts and write talismans calligraphically, aspirants are ready to lead ritual. In the People's Republic of China, some seminaries still provide formal doctrinal instruction but that is generally not the case in Taiwan.

Formal ordination focuses on the symbolism of the master's conferring the seal of priesthood and the texts the specialist will follow. Some scholars suggest the training of Black Hats is more rigorous and literate than that of the Red Turbans, who tend to serve less official, more "popular" functions and have much in common with the shamans of old.

Shinto: Shinto priesthood has historically been a hereditary occupation. Even after the government officially took over the appointment of chief priests after 1868, hereditary succession continued in many localities. Perhaps the most important ingredient in maintaining standards among Shinto officials is the main educational institution now solely responsible for the training of priests. The Kogakkan ("Imperial Hall of Learning") university near Ise was originally a public institution that closed after World War II and then reopened in 1952 as a private university. Priests-to-be study Japanese history and literature, but focus on Shinto studies, especially ritual and theology. Shinto priests are not ordained clergy strictly speaking. They are lay persons granted certification or licensure upon satisfactory completion of the seminary curriculum and its qualifying exams.

Five:

_____

Spirituality and Popular Piety

46. What do these traditions say about *ultimate spiritual reality?*

Confucianism: Two of the most important concepts that define what Confucius and his followers thought about ultimate spiritual reality are those of the Dao and Heaven *(tian).* Confucian texts do not always make clear how the two differ, and at times it seems they are virtually interchangeable. In Confucian teaching, the Dao and Heaven are generally non-personal realities that are equivalent, respectively, to a primordial or eternal cosmic law (Dao) and the source of that law (Heaven). Early Confucian texts emphasize the immanent, rather than the transcendent, aspect of the Dao. For example, Confucius is reported to have observed that the Dao is very close to human beings. The Dao is therefore accessible and knowable, but that does not mean it is not also mysterious.

Confucius did not simply deny the existence of transcendent realities, but he preferred to interpret ultimate reality from the ground up, so to speak. Many of history's great theologians have constructed their systems of thought by beginning with the existence of some divine reality and working their way down. Not Confucius. He was interested primarily in the ethical implications of traditional teachings that he had inherited. He apparently thought of Heaven as the ultimate moral authority or principle. Heaven makes its "will" known to, and through, an upright sovereign. What Heaven discloses is, in turn, the Dao. Confucius reportedly described "his" Dao as consisting of two fundamental ethical components, responsibility or loyalty *(jung)* and reciprocity *(shu).* His interpretation of the Dao and Heaven is therefore quite different from the traditional Daoist interpretation. In much of Daoist thought, the Dao has priority and gives rise to Heaven, which in turn manifests the "ten thousand things" that many people call creation or the universe.

Daoism: Daoists call the ultimate spiritual reality "Dao," the Way. Long before the formal beginnings of Daoism's various movements and schools, Chinese tradition used the term Dao as a general ethical notion implying the appropriate and moral way of acting. As so often happens when a new religious tradition enters a new cultural setting, Buddhism's arrival in China led some thinkers to talk of a Buddhist "Way" in contrast with which they began to define an indigenous Chinese Way in the sense of religious beliefs and values. Daoist philosophers emphasized the unfathomable mystery of the Dao, but they viewed it as non-personal power rather than a personal divine entity. The religious equivalent seems to have been a deity called the Great Oneness (Taiyi).

The *Daodejing*'s description of how the transcendent Dao became manifest suggests a type of emanation: Dao gave rise to the One, which produced the Two, and so on. That grand and uplifting description of the ultimate mystery still remained a bit too abstract for the majority of folks. As a result, when the first schools of religious Daoism began to formulate their beliefs, they naturally gravitated toward more concrete imagery. That included the deification of the individual long believed to represent the Way as an accessible teaching, namely, Laozi. The process also led to personification of certain essential features of the mysterious Dao in the form of the heavenly triad called the Three Pure Ones. Developments of this sort multiplied and the deities took on life stories and personalities that invited devotional interaction. In practice, the many personifications of divinity are arrayed according to an administrative structure parallel to that of the imperial bureaucracy. Religiously speaking, of course, the reality is just the other way round: the imperial institutions imitated the heavenly order of things.

Shinto: *Kami* is the most important term in Shinto spirituality and theology. Its general meaning is "high or superior being," and it can be applied to a host of spiritual presences and powers. Every *kami* is said to emanate its own distinctive divine energy or force. Among the various specific designations are the following. Nature *kami* include the deities of mountain, agriculture and bestowers of sustenance, vegetation such as sacred ancient trees, and the heavenly lights. Some deities manifest themselves as animals, such as a white bird, a deer, or a monkey. Ancestral or tutelary deities *(ujigami)* include patrons of the clans, but they can also be nature *kami*. These are associated especially with shrines in regions once under the political control of the powerful families. As has often happened in Chinese traditions, some of Japan's *kami* also originated as historical figures who became deities by dint of their leadership in a clan. Large numbers of major shrines are dedicated to such figures. Other important historical *kami* include literary figures as well.

Zoomorphic *kami* form another significant category, as represented, for example, by Inari's fox. A classification of *kami* connected with ancestor veneration and exorcism are wrathful deities and malcontent spirits called *goryo* or *onryo*. They reflect the sense of moral ambivalence Japanese discern in the spirit world. Popular belief holds such evil spirits responsible for disasters from earthquake and famine to war and political failure. Many of the great sacred sites enshrine tragic heroes who suffered political downfall. Some *kami* function as "scapegoats" in that they become the focus of popular blame for all manner of unhappy events. Japanese tradition sometimes identifies *kami* as either *ara*, wild and natural, or *niki*, placid and cultivated. In some cases, separate shrines dedicated to the two aspects of the same *kami* are located some distance apart. Another distinction is that between celestial deities *(amatsukami)* and the *kami* anciently associated with particular localities. Tradition portrays some *kami* as guests or visitors from a mysterious and faraway land called Tokoyo, perhaps an acknowledgment of their origin in Buddhism and other imported traditions.

47. Are *miracles* an important element in the spirituality of these traditions?

Confucianism: Some have described Confucian teaching as philosophical in content and religious in function. As such, Confucian tradition focuses on the role of humanity in the greater scheme of things. While not denying the existence of a divine realm or the power of beings who inhabit that realm, it emphasizes the importance of each human being's full acceptance of his or her responsibility. About the rest we cannot know in detail. What we have to work with is all the myriad small realities we confront every day. Countless wonders await anyone willing to observe carefully each detail of ordinary life. Confucius would not have approved of any approach to life that amounted to waiting for the gods to do what human beings alone are responsible for. Thus, Confucian teaching is highly realistic. It does not deny the possibility of miracles, events beyond the ordinary. It merely suggests that people who are genuinely attentive to life as it unfolds already have more than enough to occupy them.

Many devoutly religious people think of miracles as the ultimate cause for gratitude. What would Confucius have considered a cause for gratitude to Heaven? First and foremost, propriety in all of the important human relationships. In addition, he would have been grateful for the predictable workings of nature. As essential as they both are to life, neither is a sure thing. When relationships and the cosmos are as they ought to be, these are the great wonders. As for Confucius himself, though he healed no one and raised no one from the dead, he did something equally marvelous: he taught without discrimination.

Daoism/CCT: Religiously devout Chinese, whether associated with Daoism or with some form of CCT, consider asking for special favors an ordinary part of being religious. In general, however, what many readers mean by the term "miraculous" would not quite describe even apparently spectacular results of supplicatory prayer and ritual in this context. A fundamental consequence of the Yin/Yang view of life is the conviction that there is an identifiable cause of everything, whether positive or negative. All evil, illness, and suffering result from disharmony and imbalance. It is true that ordinary people cannot always put their finger on the direct cause, but ritual specialists know about these things. More important, the gods and those spiritual beings who have found the secret of immortality can assist suffering humankind by bringing about the needed balance and harmony of forces. A "miracle" in this context, therefore, might be a divine intervention for the purpose not of doing the impossible, but of helping the possible to happen more quickly and easily.

Shinto: Check the index of almost any book about Shinto and you will look in vain for the word "miracle." That does not mean the tradition is entirely without interesting analogies to what many people mean by the term. Shinto recommends regular expressions of gratitude to the *kami* for their inestimable bounty. It also recommends prayer of petition for whatever worshipers may need. Many people believe that one ordinary role of the *kami* is to make the seemingly impossible possible. In a way, that is the essence of divine power, for worshipers regard the *kami* as nurturing protectors who look after the best interests of their devotees.

48. Are *relics* significant in these traditions?

China: As important as ancestor veneration has been throughout Chinese history, one might expect relics to be a conspicuous feature in Confucian tradition. Confucians, along with Daoists, Chinese Buddhists, and practitioners of CCT, pay a great deal of attention to a variety of symbols associated with deceased ancestors. Those ancestors can be spiritual as well as biological forebears—people like Confucius and the other sages, for example. But here tradition emphasizes the spirit and values of the ancestor. People do not focus on physical remnants of the individual as though they contained the distillate of some special power. People visit the graves of outstanding figures like Confucius as well as of their departed loved ones, but they do not go in hope of some miracle as devotees of other traditions might when making pilgrimage to the site of some powerful relic. Chinese tradition reveres the simple, noble humanity and admirable personal qualities of those who have passed on. On the other hand, amulets of various kinds offer protection, and these may include the equivalent of second- or third-class relics (personal effects of a holy person, or items said to have come in contact with the holy remains).

Japan: Sacred objects play a very important role in Shinto ritual. Every shrine houses some small token of the deity who graciously calls this humble place home for the benefit of worshipers who come to pay their respects. These objects, called *goshintai* or "revered *kami* body," are said to include such unremarkable items as a mirror, sword, comb, ball of iron, paintings, pebbles, or pieces of carefully cut paper. Worshipers generally do not get even a passing glimpse of the objects, for they remain always behind the innermost shrine's closed doors. When people visit a shrine, they do so not so much because the sacred objects are there, but because the presence of the *kami* makes the place holy. When Christians or Buddhists, for example, make pilgrimage to a special church or stupa they frequently do so because certain objects associated with a particular sacred person are enshrined there. They may not believe that the objects themselves contain miraculous powers, but it is the presence of the objects that makes the place worth visiting. Shinto's sacred objects play a very different role. Many worshipers may not even be aware of exactly what items a given shrine holds. In other words, from the perspective of Shinto worshipers, the symbols of the *kami* are of secondary importance.

49. Is there such a thing as a *saint* in Chinese and Japanese religious traditions?

Confucianism: Confucius revered the ancient kings as sages *(sheng),* figures of towering intellect and virtue who represented an ideal never again to be attained by mere mortals. Their inimitability prevented the ancients from functioning as exemplars and restricted them to the role of venerable ancestors to whom all owed a debt of gratitude. Mengzi began to modify the role of the sage. He suggests that the sage appears in every age, not only in the distant past. And he emphasizes the sage's humanity and imitability. Individuals can aspire to and cultivate the qualities of the sage through education. With the Song dynasty came Neo-Confucianism and a further expansion of the sage's role. Building on the classic text called *The Great Learning (Daxue)* medieval scholars spoke of a series of stages through which an aspirant could advance toward the lofty goal of sagehood. Neo-Confucians identified the sage as the individual who had fully actualized all moral and intellectual potential and arrived at a state of oneness with the universe.

Like the Daoist sage described in the *Daodejing,* the Confucian sage embodies perfect harmony with the cosmos. Unlike the Daoist sage, the Confucian puts wisdom's insights to work by active involvement in the ordinary affairs of society. A Confucian sage is like the Buddhist bodhisattva in that both are committed to the betterment of the human condition. The ten-stage "bodhisattva career" offers a general parallel to the Neo-Confucian system of steps toward sagehood. But whereas the bodhisattva has the power to reach down and change the plight of those who ask for help, the sage offers the hope of transformation through determination and effort. Sages model the highest and best in Confucianism's spirituality of public service.

Daoism: Perhaps the closest thing in Daoism to what many people mean by the term "saint" is the ideal of human development called the sage *(zhenren).* Unlike ordinary people, the sage keeps his knowledge hidden, because there is no need to impress or persuade others. A sage is thus like the silent, unobtrusive Dao. Neither does the sage labor over the right course of action, for love is squandered when spent on specific deeds rather than lavished equally on all. The sage understands that failing to yield is not to be confused with courage. The sage knows how to give without being emptied, how to take in without being filled. Completely in harmony with nature, the sage acts without intent, learns without studying intently. Chinese religious traditions have often elevated otherwise ordinary individuals to a status above the merely human. But there is no standard formal process by which this elevation takes place.

In this respect, Daoism is closer to Islam than to Christianity, for example, where sainthood requires elaborate and lengthy investigation and verification. Emperors and others in authority have sometimes announced honors of this kind by decree, but sages are generally acknowledged to be such as a result of grass-roots movements rather than by pronouncement from on high. There is at least one other distinctive feature of the making of a Daoist sage. Whereas saints in various traditions arrive at a level of spiritual perfection typically as a result of divine grace, the Daoist sage is a product of self-help.

Three historical and five legendary persons believed to have achieved immortality figure prominently in Chinese religious lore. Daoist sources tell of many other mortals who have achieved immortality, but these "Eight Immortals" are especially important. Chinese religious lore contains many sets of eight (trigrams, precious objects, cosmic directions, for example). The Immortals *(xian)* are in some ways analogous to Christianity's saints and Islam's Friends of God. Lu Dongbin, originally a patriarch of the Perfect Realization school during the eighth century, generally leads the group. He is usually depicted dressed as a scholar carrying a fly-whisk. Some images show him with his magical sword, one of the Eight Daoist Emblems. Lu is patron of barbers and is celebrated for his healing powers. Li Tieguai, a purely legendary figure whose emblems are the gourd and crutch, appears as an old crippled beggar. He champions the weak and marginalized and is a patron of pharmacists.

Zhang Guolao lived sometime between 650 and 750 C.E. Capable of making himself invisible, Zhang appears riding (often backward!) on a white mule that he could roll up and tuck into his sleeve. His emblem is the percussion instrument made of a bamboo tube and two sticks and he is the patron of elderly men. He Xian'gu, the lone female of the group, holds a bamboo ladle, a lotus or basket of flowers, and sometimes the peach of immortality. She is said to have lived around 700 C.E. and is noted for her asceticism and kindness. Han Xiangzi is the patron of musicians. He carries a flute and was known for his spendthrift ways and delight in mountain solitude. Zhongli Chuan is supposed to have been a soldier of old who lost in battle and went off to become an alchemist. Apparently once a historical figure, the aging, portly gent eventually ascended to heaven on a stork and now carries a fan. Lan Caihe is a strange figure among strange figures. With one foot bare and one shod, sometimes appearing as a woman, sometimes as a boy, he carries a basket of flowers and is patron of florists. Cao Guojiu, patron of actors, carries a pair of castanets or, alternatively, a jade court tablet that was his entry pass and from which the image of castanets may have developed. Tradition makes this eighth Immortal the brother of a Song Dynasty empress and dresses him in royal finery. The whole octet are still widely popular and sought out for their magical powers.

Shinto: Many great and exemplary human beings have been identified and revered as *kami* after their deaths. Since the category of *kami* is an all-inclusive grouping of forces and persons considered "above" the merely human, Shinto tradition has no need of an intermediary category such as that of "saint." Most traditions that talk of sainthood in one form or another do so out of one of two convictions. In some traditions the deity is so exalted and transcendent that ordinary human beings can scarcely imagine approaching the deity directly. Saints function as intermediaries in that they share the humanity of devotees and are thus more approachable. Other traditions elevate certain persons not as intermediaries or intercessors, but as examples of lofty yet attainable perfection. Shinto stands alone here in the sense that the *kami* are everywhere and thus perfectly accessible, and that certain human beings are themselves *kami*.

50. Do these traditions celebrate the *birthdays* of any religious figures or honor them on "feast days"?

Confucianism: September 28 of each year marks the birthday of Confucius in Taiwan, for example, and there it has also been declared Teachers' Day. In the People's Republic of China, celebrations of the day have been forbidden since the Maoist revolution of 1948, largely because of Confucianism's long-standing association with imperial rule. Taiwanese celebrations are still elaborate and traditional on the day, beginning at six in the morning according to ancient practice.

Ceremonies commence with a ritual drumming followed by a procession in which participants dressed in ancient regalia carry in special symbols to welcome the spirit of Confucius. Processional symbols include a royal canopy and fan, as well as ritual long-handled axes. In the capital city, Taipei, the celebration is modeled on the ancient pattern in which Literati bureaucrats performed the main rituals. There the mayor presides over the various ranks of governmental employees and educational administrators, joined by ranks of students of different ages. Birthdays of particular deities or immortals do not play a role in Confucianism or the CIT as they do in Daoism and CCT.

Daoism/CCT: Deities both great and small are generally thought to have birthdays, because the vast majority of them were once human beings. CCT has transformed numerous figures, originally Daoist, Buddhist, and Confucian, into more comfortable characters—members of everybody's family, in effect. Other deities remain in their more exalted original Daoist forms. Here are only a few of the hundreds of divine birthday dates. Among the earliest in the year is that of the Jade Emperor, celebrated on the ninth of the first month. On the third day of the second month CCT acknowledges Wenchang Dijun, the god of literature and learning.

Guanyin's birthday occurs on the nineteenth of the second month. Xuantian Shangdi, the Supreme Emperor of Dark Heaven, was born on the third of the third month and is so celebrated in some four hundred Taiwanese temples. A quasi-Daoist deity called the Great Emperor Who Protects Life, Baosheng Dadi, is celebrated on the fifteenth of the third month. Mazu, often referred to as the Great Aunt or Grandma, has her celebration on the twenty-third of the third month. On the thirteenth day of the fifth month the general-become-deity Guandi gets his due. An otherwise anonymous City God's day is the fifteenth of the sixth month. Devotees of CCT observe the birthdays of Caojun on the third day of the eighth month, and that of Tudi Gong on the fifteenth. Also on the third of that month Daoists celebrate the birthday of Siming, the Director of Destiny, known in CCT as the Kitchen God or Hearth Deity.

Shinto: Many shrines hold special festivities in connection with dates important in the lives of enshrined *kami* who were historical figures prior to their deification. For example, the Akama Jingu enshrines the child Emperor Antoku (1178–85) who reigned for the final five years of his very brief life. From April 23 to 25, celebrants recall his untimely death and the reign of his predecessor, Emperor Gotoba. Tenjin Matsuri from July 24 to 25 celebrates the deified scholar and court minister Sugawara Michizane (845–903). Over ten thousand branch shrines ritualize the deity who is mythically associated with oxen and cattle. According to tradition, Sugawara was born and came of age in the year of the ox and was saved from his enemy by a bull who miraculously appeared to kill his would-be assassins. Ironically, it was members of that same enemy clan, the Fujiwara, who had Sugawara enshrined some fifty years after his death. He received the name Tenjin ("celestial *kami*") and has remained popular as the *kami* of learning. Sizable numbers of worshipers still arrive at his shrines on the twenty-fifth (both his birth and death day) of each month to reverence statues of reclining bulls, rubbing them and then rubbing the blessing onto themselves or their children. Birthdays are not as important on the whole as are death anniversaries and seasonal associations with the deified figures.

51. Have there been any Confucian, Daoist, or Shinto *mystics?*

Confucianism: Scholars of the history of religion rarely describe the Confucian tradition as a wellspring of mystical spirituality. But several important figures, particularly among the Neo-Confucians, spoke a language reminiscent of some of the great monistic mystics of other traditions. Zhuxi, a leading light in the Neo-Confucian School of Principle, saw in the practice of meditation a way of becoming one with cosmic harmony. Instructive parallels can be drawn between traditional descriptions of this type of meditation, and of certain qualities of the sage, and characteristics of "nature mystics" in other traditions. In Zhuxi's view, "silent sitting" promised the realistic possibility of experiencing unity with all things and all people. Wang Yangming, a later exponent of the Neo-Confucian School of Mind, talked of realizing one's "true self" in a meditative quest for enlightenment. He identified cosmic principle *(li)* with the mind, so that discovery of the true self meant discovering the ultimate reality. Some discern parallels between Wang's mysticism and that of the German mystic Meister Eckhart (c. 1260–1327 C.E.).

Daoism: Traditional accounts of many famous Daoists describe their inner experiences in terms consistent with those often associated with mysticism. A mystic, in general terms, is a human being who through a variety of ritual or devotional practices experiences spiritual transcendence. Moving out of and beyond him or herself, the mystic abides at least temporarily in a dimension very different from what most people experience most of the time. Some refer to the great Daoist figures as "nature mystics," since they enter into that different dimension by contemplating nature. They experience oneness with the cosmos intuitively rather than by reasoning their way to an intellectual conclusion. In a trance-like state, the mystic loses all sense of selfhood and individuality, becoming one with the Dao. Some have referred to the experience as the "fast of the mind" in which one listens with the ears of the spirit. What exactly the experience feels like, Daoist sources are reluctant to say, but they readily offer advice about how to cultivate the experience. By way of exception, some Daoist sources also hint that the occasional mystic has experienced a somewhat more personal form of union with the divine, akin to what Hindu and other traditions call "theistic mysticism."

Shinto: Mainstream Shinto tradition has not been particularly noted for producing important mystical figures. That is not to say that there have been no Shinto mystics. But talk of mystical union with the divine has come more from various syncretistic schools and sects, especially those heavily influenced by non-Japanese schools of religious thought. Kurozumi Munetada, founder of the Kurozumi sect with a distinctively neo-Confucian tilt, taught the importance of the deliberate quest to become a *kami.* He himself is said to have experienced oneness with the sun goddess Amaterasu when she suffused his body.

52. Has *martyrdom* ever been important in the history of the Chinese and Japanese traditions?

Confucianism: Several Confucian Literati have come to be known as martyrs. They died because those in power would not countenance their calls for greater justice in the imperial regime. One such figure was Yang Jishang (1516–1555 C.E.). So strong was his conviction that the imperial system would respond to good-faith Confucian criticism that he risked all to denounce a corrupt official at court. Yang meticulously crafted his case against Yensung and his son, fasting for three days before presenting his charges. Yensung managed to poison the emperor's mind against Yang, implicating him falsely in a conspiracy. Yang languished in prison for three years while fellow Literati attempted to defend him at court.

All appeals lost, the heroic Yang refused to take a sedative before being tortured in prison. Prior to his execution, he composed a short poem, in true Literati style. In it he expressed the hope that he would live on in spirit, still loyal to the emperor and grateful for his life of service. What is essential to note here is this martyr's dedication to advancing society through selfless commitment to justice in public administration, an outstanding feature of the Confucian spirituality of service.

Shinto: Shinto tradition reveres many religious heroes who died defending their emperor and homeland. They are martyrs in the broadest sense of the term. They died not for a religious creed narrowly defined but out of allegiance to the larger complex of beliefs that has been integral to Japanese history and culture. People like the cultural icon Sugawara Michizane, who is said to have perished as a result of his convictions, take their place alongside the royal heroes, such as the princes who died in defense of the imperial house. Shrines such as those designated as "nation-protecting" shrines are dedicated to the memory of war dead. They enshrine as *kami* the souls of all who gave their lives out of conviction. Yasukuni Jinja in Tokyo is a fine example of such a martyr memorial.

53. Do Confucians, Daoists, and adherents of Shinto believe in *angels* or *devils?*

Confucianism: Confucius and his disciples preferred not to speculate about the existence of the countless beings that in popular belief animated the spirit world. If there is good in the world, human beings can take some of the credit. When evil gets the upper hand, human beings must acknowledge their responsibility and set about reestablishing a just order. Confucian tradition does not explicitly deny that spirits, both satisfied and malevolent, regularly pass unseen and generally undetected through the lives of ordinary people. In fact, its insistence on the centrality of ancestor veneration is a clear, if implicit, acknowledgment of the spirit world. But apart from that, the tradition emphasizes the need for human beings to focus on the more immediate facts of life. Follow the example of the virtuous, strive to establish justice every day, build all relationships on honesty. There will always be events human beings cannot explain simply, and circumstances beyond human control. Some of them may be attributable to spirits, but the important thing is not to become distracted from the ongoing demands of the call to personal virtue and responsibility.

Daoism/CCT: Spirits of all kinds inhabit the ordinary world of countless adherents of Daoism and CCT. But none quite fit the precise description most readers would identify as angelic. Angels are generally understood as pure immortal spirits made that way from the start. Chinese Daoist and popular beliefs include countless immortal beings, but, apart from the highest gods, most of those began as human beings and achieved immortality later. In addition, angels in other traditions typically function as messengers or guardians. A variety of spirits play those roles in Daoist and CCT lore. Perhaps the closest thing to angels in the Chinese repertoire of religious symbolism are the *apsaras* imported into China with Buddhism.

Demonic forces abound in the spiritual universe of millions of Chinese. Many demons are the unsettled spirits of the dead who roam the world in search of their just deserts. Some demons can herald good tidings, but most are disgruntled and thirsty for vengeance. Evil spirits, called *gui,* belong to a large category distinguished from an equally large category of generally benevolent beings called *shen,* a category that includes both deities and ancestral spirits. One of the essential features of Chinese thought on these matters is the notion that there are several different kinds of soul or spirit. The heavenly "Yang soul" (called *hun*) rises at death to become a *shen* and abides from then on in heaven and in the ancestral tablets that have a prominent place on every home altar. The earthly "Yin soul" (called *po*) returns to the grave with the body. Under certain circumstances, the *po* takes a negative turn and becomes an evil spirit, a *gui,* destined to create havoc for the living. Some of these evil spirits can be particularly dangerous, but unlike the "devils" of some other traditions, the *gui* are not particularly noted for their role in tempting humans to sin.

Shinto: Perhaps the closest formal analogy to the angel in Shinto tradition are the *tennin,* the Japanese version of Buddhism's celestial nymphs called *apsaras.* They are spirits, but other than that, they do not function quite the way angels do in other traditions. Lovely celestial beings have sometimes been said to descend and dance in response to divinely beautiful music. If we focus on the functional parallels, on angels as messengers of the divine world, Shinto offers a number of analogies. But they don't "look" at all like angels. These messengers are, for example, Inari's fox and the monkey assistant of Sanno, "the mountain king." Another functional aspect of angels is that of protecting and generally mediating peace and blessing. Shinto psychology divides "soul" or "spirit" into two main types, positive and negative. *Nigimitama* are the "benign spirits" that either bestow blessing or effect spiritual changes in people or natural objects. In that sense, they function somewhat like angelic spirits, but they were not necessarily created as spirits, as angels are. They can be the spirits of the deceased that continue to roam the cosmos. A postwar sect called Byakko Shinko-kai, however, focused on a modified version of the "guardian angel" as an essential spiritual power.

Numerous demons *(oni)* inhabit the cosmos of popular Shinto belief, but their particular province is the north. They are associated with negative forces generally and bad luck. "Rough spirits" (called *aramitama*) are among the larger category of generic "spirits or souls." A category of beings called *onryo* are angry spirits, while another group of beings called *goryo,* "august spirits," are also generally troublesome but deserving of respect for their power. Some of Shinto's most important shrines are known as *goryo* shrines because the *kami* dwelling there were once human beings who died under inauspicious circumstances. Another large category of evil spirits is that of *bakemono,* a term that refers to several different specific groups of beings especially prevalent in folklore.

54. Given the ubiquitous presence of spirits, is *exorcism* an important practice in Chinese or Japanese traditions?

Confucianism/CIT: Shamans of ancient times and their Daoist successors, the Black Hat and Red Turban ritual specialists, have generally played the role of exorcists to the Chinese population at large. Confucians and members of the imperial administration might very well have enlisted the services of an exorcist in particular instances. But neither Confucianism nor the CIT focuses on matters of this kind, except in relation to ancestor veneration rituals. In a way, attending to the spirits of the dead, whether of the individual family or of the imperial dynasty, seeks to obviate the need for exorcism as such. Proper, sincere, and timely acknowledgment of those spirits reduces the likelihood that frustrated souls will wander abroad with mischievous intent.

Daoism/CCT: Many Daoist rituals are designed to expel, control, or pacify troublesome spirits, or, by extension, to banish drought, famine, or outlaws who might have been plaguing the local citizenry. Daoists rarely identify individual problems as personal cases of demonic *(gui)* possession. Much more common are instances in which a specialist's skills are required to liberate temples, homes, and business establishments from evil influences. Until some thirty years ago, Roman Catholic tradition included a specific ritual to ordain young candidates for the priesthood to the Order of Exorcist, one of four so-called "minor orders." Ordination to the Daoist priesthood still includes an emphasis on the ability to perform exorcism as one of its essential features.

Rare descriptions of demonic possession suggest some elements similar to those found in Roman Catholic archival accounts of exorcism, including the occasional need to have several stout attendants restrain the possessed person. After performing a variety of ritual actions, such as lighting candles and incense and burning the appropriate charm, the exorcist enjoins the spirit to depart and a contest of wills ensues. More common, indeed regularly scheduled, rites of temple purification may include dramatization of an encounter between the offending demon and the deity called Chung Kuei, dispatcher of demons. After the demon (sometimes played by a member of the temple staff or a professional actor) steals an incense burner, the priest/deity subdues the evil one and returns the stolen item to the temple gods. Only through the dominance of Yang over Yin can a successful exorcism be carried out. The climactic moment occurs as the high priest drives the evil spirit out to the accompaniment of intense sound from percussion instruments. Another method for ridding a building of the evil presence is to create billows of holy smoke by boiling oil and adding water to it.

Shinto: Demons and assorted evil influences miss no opportunity to make a nuisance of themselves, especially at times when human beings and natural processes are most vulnerable. Beginnings, such as planting time or the birth of an infant, can be particularly difficult in this respect. Shinto tradition includes various understandings of how evil forces work and several methods for contending with them. Most undesirable forces are associated with impurity and pollution. Some evil spirits will depart in a ritual that designates as a scapegoat any animal or object capable of taking on the negative forces. Emperors of old would rub a human effigy over their bodies, leaving all personal impurity on the image, which officials of the "Bureau of Yin and Yang" then ritually consigned to a river.

Some rituals use a weapon such as a sword to attack the evil power as though it were a physical presence. Other rituals assume the evil forces have taken on demonic bodies and must be pursued and expelled from a locality. In one rite, people throw soybeans in unlucky directions and command the demons to depart, an important element of the Spring Setsubun ("Season Change") Matsuri. Some large festivals are entirely dedicated to a type of communal exorcism. An originally Buddhist rite called Goryoe ("Meeting with August Spirits") has been associated with Kyoto's famous Gion Matsuri, for example. That festival arose out of a need to banish the spirits of disease and eventually grew into a full-scale Shinto celebration. Another important interpretation of spirit possession has been traditionally associated with the belief that the fox is capable of changing shapes. Extraordinary spiritual states were therefore sometimes explained as a type of "fox-possession." Some popular traditions identify various psychosomatic illnesses as forms of possession. "Soul Pacification" (Tamashizume) is a sort of reverse exorcism in which ritualists seek to make a spirit content to remain in the body of a person suffering from illness.

55. What role do *dreams* and *visions,* or other spirit-manifestations, play?

Confucianism/CIT: Popular and official religious practices cross over when it comes to dreams and visions. Confucian tradition sees relatively little value in such experiences, except insofar as they reveal an individual's state of mind. But Chinese tradition generally puts considerable credence in these alternative and privileged ways of arriving at the truth. For example, emperors were often said to have had dreams informing them of the proper course of action with respect to religious matters. Local CIT magistrates who experienced difficulty in deciding on legal cases were instructed to stay overnight in the temple of the local "spirit magistrate" who would deliver the answer in a dream.

Daoism/CCT: An ability to interpret the dreams of ordinary folk has long been part of the ritual menu of Chinese religious specialists, beginning with the shamans of old. In ancient times, experts called *zhanren* interpreted dreams using divination and astrology as their tools. Powerful and famous people, too, report having revelatory dreams that move them toward a new course of action. Dream accounts therefore frequently function as instruments of divine or spiritual legitimation. There is often a very fine line between dream and vision, except that one can experience a vision while awake. Religiously important visions or dreams frequently feature major deities, such as Laozi or the Jade Emperor, who deliver instructions or revelations to the dreamer or visionary. In addition, visualization techniques figure prominently in the meditative practice of some Daoist schools. The Shangqing school, for example, recommends that the meditator focus imaginatively on his or her indwelling deities, a technique similar to that used by several Tibetan Buddhist schools. By conjuring up intricate detail as described in the school's sacred texts, the meditator makes the presence of the god real and can thus unite with the divine presence.

Shinto: Shinto legends tell countless tales of how famous figures have enjoyed—or barely survived—encounters with the spirit world. Many religiously prominent individuals claimed to have received divine visitations and privileged communications in dreams. Various spirits, even evil ones called *goryo,* are capable of making their presence known for the purpose of delivering an oracle. These spirits are also called "living human *kami*" *(arahitogami),* who can return in their human form to make things both positive and negative happen in the land of the living. Famous people who died untimely or violent deaths, such as Prince Shotoku Taishi (574–622) and poet-calligrapher Sugawara Michizane (845–903) to whom over ten thousand shrines are dedicated, later became *kami* and could exert unhappy influence if not dealt with properly. This is a striking amalgam of positive and negative powers in one spirit, for such a spirit can manifest itself in frightening apparitions as well as in blessings.

56. Is the practice of *divination* prominent in Chinese and Japanese spiritualities?

Confucianism/CIT: Two types of divination have been important ingredients in the ritual life of both Confucianism and the CIT. As in Daoism and CCT, the practice of geomancy (earth-prognostication) called *fengshui* has always been a necessary prerequisite for the siting and planning of all structures, from the humblest home to the grandest temple or palace. Those contemplating any building project would enlist a specialist in *fengshui* for a thorough reading of the natural characteristics of the proposed site. In addition, people from the emperor on down regularly consult specialists in interpreting the oracles of the *Yijing,* the *Classic of Change,* before undertaking any significant course of action. The imperial staff retained experts in divination available on short notice. These specialists were not specifically members of the Literati or Confucian hierarchies, but their services were generally regarded as indispensable.

Daoism/CCT: Divinatory rites are more critical to Daoism and CCT than to many other major traditions. Long before Daoism came into being as a distinct set of traditions, the Chinese practiced divination through the stars, yarrow sticks, oracle bones, and tortoise shells. Important types of divination are the celestial, the terrestrial, interpretations of events and omens, and the forecasting of individual destinies. Celestial divination, a variety of astrological interpretation, plots the locations of stars according to one of the twelve "palaces" associated with the lunar month of one's birth, in order to understand a host of factors including sickness and health, luck, family issues, and personality. Terrestrial divination uses an elaborate geomantic compass to assist practitioners in aligning their lives most effectively with the forces of nature. All ordinary events in the life of each person have their hidden meanings, and special divinatory skills allow one to interpret the nature of the energy played out in all happenings, in relation to the specific time of day or year.

Some occurrences clearly have ominous qualities and require specialized interpretative skills. Thunder or lightning and other natural events suggest forces that set them aside from more mundane happenings. Perhaps the most important and widespread forms of divination are those that help people divine their personal destinies. Some focus on reading physical features, such as the shapes of facial characteristics or palm lines. Here we are moving away from strictly Daoist teaching and into popular practice.

Shinto: *Bokusen* is the Japanese term for the complex process of divining auspicious times for agriculturalists. Divination encompasses a variety of specific devices. As in CCT, people often draw lots—the Chinese shake bundles of numbered sticks and pull the one left protruding, and Shinto worshipers draw numbered bits of paper. Sometimes they will read the angle at which an arrow sticks in its target, or read the designs on a turtle shell, or hold a deer's shoulder blade in a flame and observe how it cracks. (A similar ritual uses arrows for slightly different purposes. People can purchase white arrows at shrine shops especially around the New Year and use them as amulets or protective devices at home during the rest of the year.) Divination is required for setting the dates for many major festivals. Ritual leaders invite certain divinatory *kami* to be in attendance as the diviner kindles a sacred fire on which a turtle shell will be heated. Diviners then read the relationship of the cracks to the lines and characters that have been pre-drawn on the shell.

A ritual cousin of Chinese *fengshui* is called *kaso*. It involves a set of geomantic calculations to establish optimal conditions for all sorts of human habitations. Another type of divination has worshipers write on small pieces of paper various options open to them as they prepare to make a major decision. In a variation on a contemporary popular Chinese practice, people typically pull a stick from amidst a bundle of them, read its number, and take a piece of pre-printed advice from a correspondingly numbered drawer. Numerous Shinto shrines provide racks where people who find the advice unpalatable can tie their paper to be rid of the effects of the bad news.

57. How do Chinese and Japanese faith traditions deal ritually with *death* and *mourning?*

Confucianism/CIT: Confucian practices associated with funerals and ancestor veneration are of a piece with those of Daoism and CCT in that the basic elements are common to most segments of traditional Chinese societies. Confucius and his disciples did have some specific thoughts on the matter, though. The disciple Xunzi wrote that the feelings of loss and longing for a deceased person, and the ritual expression of those feelings, represented the height of human civilization and culture. In a way, one knows the humanity of others through the attachment they express to lost loved ones. Although Confucius himself declined to speculate about the experience of death or the condition of one who has died, he seems to have felt strongly that there were appropriate ritual and emotional responses. When asked whether he recommended the full three-year period of mourning, Confucius responded that if Literati whose loved ones died were to dispense with the practice, they would risk the irrevocable loss of some of society's most important rituals. He added that if the questioner felt comfortable performing only a year's grieving, he might do so. After the questioner had left, however, the Teacher commented on how heartless that person must have been. Parents attend to their infants unceasingly for three years. The least their children can do is return the favor symbolically.

One specific issue that has historically been very important for Confucianism and the CIT is the question of monumental funereal architecture and special memorials for the great and powerful. Confucius and several of the tradition's later teachers have been remembered with fairly modest grave markers. Tombs of emperors, on the other hand, have often been grand, even extravagant, architectural works. At least one ruler even commissioned a virtual reconstruction of the royal residence underground (in Xi'an), complete with thousands of life-size terra-cotta soldiers to protect the imperial remains.

Daoism/CCT: Specific rites are designed for those approaching death, for burial day, and for subsequent memorials. For the elderly and terminally ill, ceremonies can include rituals related to aging and particular illnesses. Prayers for longevity might include, for example, recitation from the scripture called *The Northern Dipper's Extension of Life.* Traditional funerals conducted under Daoist auspices can be very elaborate. At many funerals, a central feature is the recitation of scripture often performed, curiously, by Buddhist monks or nuns. Many Chinese, both in China and in places like Malaysia where there are sizable

Chinese communities, still choose to bury their dead in distinctive graves. A horseshoe shaped stone or concrete enclosure is set into a gentle slope with the open side to the south and the arms of the "horseshoe" inclining toward the south. Following the principles of *fengshui,* the enclosure helps to contain the maximum positive *qi* while allowing necessary drainage. Burial ceremonies typically involve placing a memorial or name tablet atop the coffin during final prayers. The coffin is then buried, head to the south, within the semi-circular enclosure.

Family members take the tablet home for installation on the domestic altar. Weekly rituals held from the seventh to the forty-ninth day after death may be even more complex than that of the actual burial. Salvation rituals are especially important in cases of violent or premature death. In order to liberate such unfortunate souls, a ritual of "crossing over" is designed to shatter the very portals of the underworld. The so-called Ghost Festival, held either at the end of a Cosmic Renewal or on the fifteenth day of the seventh month, placates the "hungry spirits" with often elaborate offerings and animal sacrifice presided over by seven officiants. For those who died before being able to marry, posthumous "spirit marriages" engage a living proxy to marry the deceased person symbolically, while allowing the proxy to proceed with his or her marriage plans in due course.

Shinto: According to a well-known saying, "Shinto marries, Buddhism buries." During the Tokugawa era (1600–1867) an imperial decree stipulated that only Buddhist priests should conduct funeral rites. Most cemeteries in Japan are connected to Buddhist temples rather than Shinto shrines. There are exceptions to that general rule, however, and practitioners of Shinto have important beliefs and rituals having to do with death and mourning. A major difference between Buddhist and Shinto practices is that Shinto rites never occur in primary ritual spaces, for shrines are strictly dedicated to the *kami,* and adherents of Shinto regard death as a form of evil and a serious source of pollution.

Shinto belief and practice have been profoundly influenced by certain Confucian attitudes toward departed ancestors, and large numbers of Japanese still perform rites of ancestor veneration. Some Japanese families follow the practice of enshrining a deceased person's symbols in a "spirit house" *(tamaya),* placed beneath the home's miniature shrine *(kamidana),* seven weeks after a funeral. Some of Japan's largest shrines are dedicated to memorializing the spirits of great human beings elevated to the status of *kami.* Grief *(kibuku)* is associated with a prescribed period during which the experience of death renders family members impure. Worshipers should stay away from shrines and refrain from Shinto ritual generally during that interval. In pre-Buddhist times, the Japanese sometimes constructed monumental memorials to the dead. Historically it was lay people who performed Shinto funeral rituals, with the main participants wearing white. Today, Shinto rites led by priests occur in homes or funeral establishments, while some shrines continue to perform memorial rites for those who have died in battle.

Six:

Religion and Artistic Expression

58. Are there any signs or symbols that might *identify an individual* as an adherent of a particular Chinese or Japanese tradition?

Confucianism: Confucian tradition consists far more of actions and the preservation of proper relationships than of the expression of specific doctrines. The tradition so pervades Chinese and other Asian cultures that it is like the air one breathes rather than a distinct set of beliefs. As a result, it is virtually impossible to tell who among Chinese, Japanese, or Koreans think of themselves as Confucians. There are still some people who identify themselves exclusively or even primarily as disciples of the Master, but they are relatively few in number. Since so many rituals that Chinese and other east Asians perform are common to members of various religious traditions, the fact that an individual practices ancestor veneration, for example, offers no clues in this regard. There are, however, a number of symbols that are connected with daily life originally associated with Confucius and that still appear in popular arts of Asia. The so-called "Four Treasures of the Literary Apartment," for example, include an ink stick, ink block, brush, and paper.

Daoism/CCT: Symbols associated with religious beliefs and folk practices abound in societies heavily influenced by Chinese culture. Over the centuries, the major Chinese religious traditions—Daoist, Confucian, Buddhist, and popular—have shared many of those symbols and signs. Overlapping of symbols of various traditions makes it difficult if not impossible to know at a glance to which tradition the owner and user of the symbols belongs. Signs and symbols generally associated with CCT include a vast range of protective and magical devices, amulets, and talismans. Perhaps the most widely used symbol is that of the perfect harmony of Yin and Yang. Appearing on all sorts of personal items such as rings and pendants, the so-called *taiji* (Supreme Ultimate) is a circle in which two equal but opposite curving tear-shapes embrace. In other words, an S-curve line divides the circle in two equal parts. The darker half symbolizes Yin, the brighter half Yang, but the commingling of the two is symbolized by a dark dot in the larger end of the Yang shape and a corresponding bright dot in the Yin shape.

Sometimes, as on the national flag of South Korea, that symbol is surrounded by four of the eight trigrams *(bagua)*. The trigrams are made up of combinations of solid Yang lines and broken Yin lines. Charm-like devices are extremely popular in Chinese societies. Textiles and other decorative items, like ceramic wares, invariably display a range of symbolic features. Symbols they might show can include any of dozens of animal, plant, or inanimate objects associated with aspects of the greatest mysteries of life, of those things that human beings most hope for or fear. For example, the tortoise and crane mean long life, the dragon means protection, the phoenix warmth. The heron and countless other birds of good omen betoken happiness, while creatures of ill omen, such as the owl, portend death and bad fortune.

Shinto: Apart from times of participation in public or private rituals, it is virtually impossible to identify practitioners of Shinto on the basis of personal symbolism. When people join in festival processions, many don small jackets called *happi,* which extend to about mid-thigh, and headbands. *Happi* sometimes bear the logo of the local association that carries the *mikoshi* portable shrine in processions. On special days, young women may dress up in their best *kimono.* Devotees sometimes return home from shrines carrying amulets or talismans, but these items are visible less often on the person than in the home.

59. What signs or symbols distinguish *ritual specialists* in the Chinese and Japanese traditions?

Confucianism/CIT: Even in today's post-imperial world, leaders of Confucian rituals are typically also government officials. When they function as ritual specialists, they don the garments once worn by representatives of the imperial household and administration. As for the CIT, since there is no longer any official imperial religious worship, there are no longer CIT ritual specialists. Prior to 1911, however, CIT ritualists, from the emperor on down to the humblest assistant, simply wore the garments that signified their respective bureaucratic ranks and offices. In this case, the Literati did double duty as custodians of both civil and religious ritual. For especially important events, officials wore various garments known generically as "dragon robes," each decorated with emblems of the wearer's administrative rank. Imperial robes worn by the ruler during rituals were once festooned with an array of symbolic decorative motifs known collectively as "The Twelve Ornaments (or Symbols)." Symbolizing heaven and its wisdom were the sun, shown with a three-legged raven inside its red disc; the blue or green moon surrounding a hare grinding the elixir of immortality with mortar and pestle; and the constellations.

Images of mountains symbolized earth and strength. Standing for all living things, the dragon symbolized resilience; the pheasant, culture and literary accomplishment. In images of bronze ritual vessels celebrants saw filial devotion, in cereal grains abundant harvest, in flame illumination, and in the water plant purity. Along with the mountains, the latter four also corresponded with the five elements. Finally, the *fu,* a geometric form meaning good fortune, and the axe referred respectively to the imperial prerogatives of judgment and punishment. When displayed together, the twelve were arranged in combinations of the five symbolic colors associated with the five directions. None but the emperor's ritual vestments could depict all twelve ornaments, since they comprised a symbolic summary of the whole cosmos.

Daoism/CCT: Daoist "priests" or "masters" make extensive use of symbolic vestments in ritual settings. Apparently in imitation of the garments emperors once wore for religious rituals, Daoist specialists today wear three types of vestments in various colors, depending on sectarian affiliation. For the most sacred occasions, a high priest wears a square red silk poncho-like vestment called the "garment of descent" that symbolizes earth. For regular major rituals, the celebrants might wear a red or yellow silk over-garment called the "Dao Gown" with the character for *taiji* or the eight trigrams on front and back. Other common decorative motifs include images of the Eight Immortals, often depicted on the hems of broad, flowing sleeves.

Abstract cloud designs often stand for Yin while cranes and male versions of the mythical creature called the *qilin* (sometimes associated with the unicorn, but very different from the European unicorn) represent Yang. For penitential rites, the assistants might wear the "sea-blue" vestment whose darker color accords with a darker ritual purpose. Under these garments specialists wear a square silk apron. Officiants also wear distinctive headgear, including a black skullcap under a metal five-pointed crown (recalling the five elements) bestowed in the ordination ceremony. Ritual shoes like those once worn in the imperial court bear cloud symbolism that suggests the ability to walk the very heavens as the priest conveys the prayers of the people to the deities.

Shinto: Shinto priests wear distinctive garb (called *shozoku*) modeled on courtly fashions from the Heian period, the days when Japan's capital was in Kyoto. Ritual robes are of several types. Priests wear a kimono and a kind of very full-cut pants underneath. Outer garments originally indicated courtly rank with various colors (robin's egg blue, red, purple, yellow, and light green) but now a priest's rank is indicated by either pale blue, black, or red. Outer garments have very wide flowing sleeves and extend down to the feet. For ordinary ceremonies, priests wore a white silk vestment called a *karinigu* ("hunting cloak" from medieval times). With the simpler garments for ordinary duties, priests wear a plain roundish hat called *eboshi,* reserving the taller and more elegant *kanmuri* for special ceremonies. Upper-rank priests wear polished wooden shoes for rituals, and their subordinates wear thong sandals of wood. During all ceremonies, officiants carry a slender, tapered slab of wood called the *shaku* in the right hand, similar to the one images of Chinese ancestor figures often carry. Since even a lay person sometimes leads rituals and wears these same garments, they do not function like a "habit" to distinguish priests from laity. When not performing their shrine duties, Shinto priests wear ordinary street clothes. Shrine maidens *(miko)* who are performing shrine duties wear a white kimono top and a vermilion or scarlet split skirt. Musicians, whether priests or not, also wear similar versions of Heian court fashion during ceremonies.

60. Is there such a thing as *Confucian* or *Shinto art* or *aesthetics?*

Confucian: A number of Confucian Literati have been credited with some of China's finest landscape paintings. They were particularly attracted to this artistic theme and medium because both were consistent with deep-rooted Confucian values. Images of mystic mountain settings shared scroll space with equally haunting poems that reflected on human life and the grandeur of nature. These visual and literary images were sometimes autobiographical in tone, offering insight into the creator's personal spiritual convictions. Paintings often depicted solitary scholars lost in contemplation of natural beauty, meditating on moonrise, or creating calligraphy in a mountain pavilion. Here Confucian tradition crosses paths with classic Daoist views of nature and with the spontaneous and abstract landscapes painted by Chan Buddhist monks. Painting and poetry became forms of meditation for the Literati, expressions of their holistic view of the balance and harmony of nature. Literati painting is a didactic art with ethical impact, for ideally it expresses the feelings of the superior person. Confucian theory accords visual art the ability to communicate ideas too delicate or too forceful for words. The mind of the artist takes precedence over the content of the work, for the ultimate benefit of a great work is that it offers a connection with a person who represents the highest moral values. Great art can arise only out of genuine virtue.

Shinto: Every twenty years, priests and specially skilled carpenters gather at the Grand Shrine at Ise for a ritual that says a lot about Shinto artistic sensibilities. They construct a new inner shrine on a plot left vacant for the previous twenty years. Then they dismantle the older shrine separated by only a small partition and leave its space empty until it is time to rebuild there. The carpenters use only the finest cypress, fashioned with the simplest of tools, and use no nails, adhesives, or artificially produced material of any kind. Each stroke of the plane or hammer is part of an ancient ritual that blends religious reverence and awe with the practical demands of sacred architecture. Each structure, however small and humble, is a work of sacred craftsmanship. During the middle ages, Shinto sculptors created anthropomorphic images of various *kami,* largely under the influence of Buddhism's rich iconography. Some sculptures remain important symbols in a few individual devotional cults within Shinto (such as Sanno Ichijitsu, with its images of the *kami*'s monkey messengers). But, on the whole, modern Shinto worship is aniconic, focusing on the presence of symbolic objects, such as the mirror and sword, within the holy of holies. One unique and historically important art form is the so-called shrine mandala. Stylized depictions of individual shrines arranged on a hanging scroll serve as a meditative device. Members of certain sects have used these mandalas as devotional focuses of esoteric contemplative rituals. Above all, shrines and their settings remain the most important visual expression of Shinto beliefs and values. Simple, natural beauty is the key.

61. Do *Confucians* mark their *sacred spaces* with any distinctive signs and symbols?

Though they are usually less flamboyant in their decor than other Chinese temples, Confucian temples typically sport a variety of intriguing iconographic details. When you enter the outer garden courtyard of the Taipei Confucian temple, you notice on its outer wall several traditional Chinese symbols: a pair of dragon-fish called *jiwen* (of which a total of fourteen protect the temple from fire—dragons bring rain and the fish symbolizes water as well) and a pair of exuberant green dragons. On the north face of the garden's south wall is a large tile image of the *qilin* (unicorn).

Writhing dragons are the principal motif in the main hall, both on the roofline and two main front columns and around the main altar, where nine of the creatures guard the spirit tablet of the Master. A pair of carved "sky pillars" appear to protrude at either end of the main hall's central ridge beam. Some say they symbolize both Confucian ethics, which alone can support the firmament, and the chimneys in which many scholars hid their books during Qin emperor Shihuangdi's attempt to burn all the texts of the Literati. In the center of that same roof beam, a small seven-roofed pagoda may symbolize the axis of the universe, standing as it does directly over the altar dedicated to Confucius himself. In rows along the beams of the sloping eaves stand birds of prey, for, according to tradition, even the fiercest raptors alighted and paused to listen when Confucius taught.

Beneath the eaves of the main hall are numerous small carved figures of popular Chinese characters, such as Shou Lao, deity of longevity. Even smaller carved friezes around the upper walls of the main hall depict scenes of high virtue from popular Chinese stories. In front of the door to Confucius's altar, at the base of the platform supporting the memorial hall, stands a stone carving of the dragon that symbolizes the emperor. Inside, the octagonal cupola over the main altar shows the eight trigrams arrayed around the circular symbol of Yin and Yang, the *taiji*.

62. Are there symbolic dimensions in *CIT sacred spaces?*

Imperial temples and altars have been highly symbolic down to the smallest detail. First, their placement in relation to each other and to the royal residence was critical. In imperial Beijing, for example, the Forbidden City stood at the center of the center of empire, which in turn was the center of the universe. Within the palace, arranged along its central north-south axis, is a succession of ceremonial halls. Beginning in the north and moving southward are the Palace of Earthly Peace, the Palace of Heavenly Brightness, the Hall of Protecting Harmony, the Hall of Middle Harmony, and the Hall of Supreme Harmony. On north-south and west-east axes stood pairs of sacred spaces balancing Yin and Yang forces.

North of the Forbidden City was the Altar of Earth (Yin), square in shape. Its counterpart due south of that below the palace was the complex centered on the round Altar of Heaven (Yang) and its various related temple and other ritual buildings. West of the Forbidden City stood the Altar of the Moon (Yin) in its square enclosure and, to the east, the Altar of the Sun (Yang) in its round-edged enclosure. These four spaces are considerable distances (say, about two miles) from the palace. But immediately south of the palace, on either side of the north-south axis that leads out of the Forbidden City and into today's Tiananmen square, the Altar of Land and Grain stood to the west across from the imperial ancestral temple.

A good example of structural symbolism is the Altar of Land and Grain's division into five sections, recalling both the directions and the five elements. Different colored earth, brought from the corners and center of the empire, filled each section: yellow in the center, black in the north, red in the south, azure or green in the east, and white in the west. That structure and its companion ancestral temple were located between the Meridian Gate, which marks the southern extremity of the Forbidden City, and Tiananmen, the Gate of Heavenly Peace, which marks the northern perimeter of the square that bears its name.

One of the most important symbolic pairs, in architectural decoration as well as in the smaller arts, is that of the dragon and the phoenix. Often depicted as though engaging in a heavenly ballet, they symbolize the harmonious relationship between the emperor (dragon) and empress (phoenix). The intertwined pair of celestial beings appears regularly on the interior oculus (center peak) of domes in Confucian and imperial temples especially.

Dragon and phoenix also appear often on the rounded ends of roof tiles. Such symbols were not allowed as decoration on any but imperial structures. Since the emperor was considered the Son of Heaven (Tianzi), you might expect various types of imagery associated with the firmament, and abstract cloud forms are among the favorites.

63. Are *Daoist and CCT sacred spaces* marked with any distinctive signs and symbols?

It is not always possible to determine from a Chinese sacred space's exterior design and decor to which of the religious traditions it belongs. Mosques (including those in Chinese settings) have their distinctive minarets, churches have their spires and crosses, and Hindu temples have their monumental facades and towers marking inner shrines. Some Chinese Buddhist temples announce their identity with pagodas or stupas, but that is not always the case. Chinese temple rooflines often display colorful small figures that appear to be engaged in vigorous action, but even these are not a reliable indicator of the holy place's specific religious affiliation. The animated figures on the rooflines sometimes illustrate scenes taken from Chinese opera or classical novels, chosen here because they allude to certain important moral virtues.

Inside the temple more specific clues are available, but even there one has to look carefully to distinguish the sacred symbols of Daoism from those of CCT. For example, a statue of the bodhisattva Guanyin (originally Buddhist) may appear on a small altar under the covered area toward the front of the inner courtyard, but that does not mean this is a Buddhist temple. It does, however, indicate that this is not a Daoist temple and probably belongs to CCT, which has assimilated Guanyin from Buddhism and made her an important deity. A Daoist temple's most distinctive symbol is its main altar. Although the overall setting varies from one sect to another, there are several important common features. Before the central deity on the altar stands a perpetually lit lamp symbolizing wisdom and the light of the Dao. Two candles symbolizing sun and moon flank the lamp a few inches farther toward the front of the altar. Cups of water (Yang), tea (Yin), and uncooked rice (Yang and Yin united) stand before the candles. Closer to the front of the altar stand five plates of fruit, each of a different color, symbolizing the five elements in perfect proportion. Centered near the front stands an incense burner, a reminder of the heat that purifies the three vital energies symbolized by three sticks of incense. Some temporary sacred spaces are constructed of bamboo for specific seasonal Daoist rituals.

64. Do *Shinto* practitioners mark their *sacred spaces* with any distinctive signs and symbols?

Easily the most important symbol of Shinto sacred spaces is the *torii* gate. Marking the entry and pathways to every shrine, *torii* typically consist of a pair of unadorned upright columns and a pair of cross beams (or lintels) at the top. The upper cross beam generally sits directly atop the column and protrudes on both sides, while the lower either ends at the columns or goes through and protrudes. Some have more elaborate uprights and cross beams, depending on local and regional architectural styles. Devotees give *torii* as votive offerings to some shrines, lining pathways with hundreds of them inches apart so that the entry to the shrine feels almost like a covered walkway. According to legend, the *torii* recalls the perch from which birds sang to entice the sun goddess from her cave.

Most Shinto shrines use the simplest and most natural materials available, imitating nature as much as possible. Natural wood grains and the lovely green forest patina that eventually accents thatch or wood-shingled roofs give them a rustic character and charm. Many shrine roofs still display remnants of primitive architectural elements as a reminder of antiquity. Even though newer building methods no longer require them structurally, many shrines retain a row of logs called *katsuogi* set along the ridge beam of the roof. Older structures needed the *katsuogi* to hold the thatch roof down. Another bit of architectural nostalgia is the vertical extensions of the eave-beams above the roof line. As you view a shrine from either front or rear, you notice that the roof line forms an X-shape. Horizontally trimmed upper ends of these beams, known as *chigi,* mark the shrines of female *kami,* and vertically trimmed ends those of male *kami.*

Several rather mysterious symbols adorn holy places, whether or not a site has a structure on it. Thick straw ropes called *shimenawa* mark sacred places such as trees and rocks. Outer portals of shrines, whether actual buildings or miniature models used on home altars, also suspend *shimenawa* across their facades. Attached to the rope are pieces of white paper cut in zigzag fashion symbolizing offerings to the *kami.* The same bits of paper are attached to a ritual wand called the *gohei.* Legend has it that the rope originated as a way of restraining the sun goddess from escaping back into her cave.

The main architectural and ritual elements of a major Shinto shrine include various symbolic dimensions. At the heart of a major shrine is a complex of three units called the *hongu* (for a *jingu, honsha* for a *jinja*). This central area, all oriented to the south as in Chinese sacred structures, houses the shrine's principal deity. Within the *hongu* are the *haiden, heiden,* and *honden* arranged front-to-rear along the south-north central axis. The outer and most public of the spaces is called the *haiden* or worship hall, where devotees gather individually or in small groups for blessings and other rituals. Most people who come to the shrine without prior arrangements for ceremonial ministrations from the priestly staff perform their brief prayers in front of the *haiden.* But if the staff are performing rituals inside, those outside are welcome to observe. From that hall, worshipers can look across an interior courtyard to the central structure, the *heiden* or offering hall, where only the priestly staff perform more sacred rituals. From there, in turn, the celebrants can see (sometimes across yet another courtyard) the *honden,* the Shinto equivalent of the "holy of holies." There, behind closed doors and visible to no one, the *kami* reside. Also on the grounds of many large shrines one may find subordinate shrines called *bekku,* which house related major deities, and *massha* for lesser deities. Some shrines also have small Buddhist temples (called *jinguji,* "shrine-temples") on the property, remnants of ancient connections between the two traditions.

65. Do *numbers, colors,* or *elements of nature* have symbolic meaning in the Chinese traditions?

Confucianism/CIT: In Confucian tradition and the CIT, as well as in other Chinese traditions generally, a set of five colors has symbolic associations. Colors are paired with the five elements (wood, water, earth, metal, fire) and directions: yellow or gold in the center, black in the north, red in the south, green or azure in the east, and white in the west. Red and gold are particularly important in the decoration of Confucian temples as reminders of the south and center. At the Temple of Heaven, the color azure and a kind of turquoise or aquamarine decorate the domed vault, suggesting an association of those colors with heaven. The Forbidden City is often described as a "purple" palace, connecting that color with royal power. Carpets spread out before the various thrones were typically yellow, the color for the center. Throughout the palace, roof tiles were yellow and columns red. Only the emperor's buildings could sport gold tiles. Red and gold were also the principal colors of royal garments, reminders of the fire at the heart of the empire.

Daoism/CCT: Astrological calculation and cosmological imagery have long been an integral part of Chinese religious views. Hundreds of symbolic elements make up this vast system of correspondences. Here are just a few samples. Zodiacal animals are associated with the twelve months. Each of the four quadrants of the universe has its seven constellations in addition to its connection with specific trigrams, all related to particular aspects of good fortune or difficulty. Each of these elements is further coordinated with one of the five symbolic colors (black, white, red, green, yellow) and elements (wood, water, earth, metal, fire) and organs of the human body.

Here are some examples of popular animal symbolism: the crow, surprisingly perhaps, symbolizes the sun. The crane, the guide of the Immortals, means long life as do the dove and the hare. Fish are reminders of renewal of life and abundance. By association with plowing new fields, the ox means spring and vitality. The sharp-eyed quick-tongued parrot looks after faithfulness in marriage.

Flowers, trees, and fruits almost always have some symbolic resonance. The springtime peony means tenderness and womanly beauty, as does the jasmine. Plum means winter and is a reminder of Laozi who was born beneath a plum tree. Bamboo betokens endurance, the orange benevolence. A complete listing would fill several books. Of course, not everyone thinks consciously of specific symbolic meanings upon seeing any of the hundreds of visual decorative motifs in the full catalogue. But most Chinese still grow up surrounded by countless symbolic associations of this kind.

66. Are *statues and other visual imagery* important in Daoist and CCT temples?

With the notable exception of major Confucian and Imperial temples, Chinese ritual spaces are almost always filled with images of deities and other sacred figures. Principal deities occupy main altar spaces, but they often share the central spot with smaller images of other sacred figures arranged below the main image and toward the front of the altar. For many centuries Daoists and practitioners of CCT evidently felt no need for anthropomorphic depictions of their deities. The advent of Buddhism, with its growing iconographic repertoire, seems to have been an important factor in the development of Chinese religious representational imagery.

Images of Daoist deities, and of those that originated outside of Daoist circles but are often identified as Daoist by association, run a wide gamut. Some of the deities are of divine origin. Others began as human beings, either historical or legendary, and achieved divine status either in life or after death. In addition to statues, colorful banners, low relief in stone and other media, and mural paintings depict mythological and other scenes meant to keep the worshiper in the proper frame of mind. Even temples that began as Buddhist institutions and that still display distinctively Buddhist imagery in their main shrines and altars have often become transformed into CCT temples by accretion over the centuries. Whatever the individual deity's life story, anthropomorphic images abound.

By far the majority of Daoist and CCT images of sacred figures are portrayed with identifiably human bodies. They rarely have multiple heads or limbs, but they do display various iconographic clues. Deities are more often than not somber, sometimes of downright forbidding countenance, and typically depicted in such a way that the viewer is not likely to think of them as ordinary human beings. Bright red or yellow skin, flaring nostrils, a riveting gaze, and the occasional menacing gesture discourage the too-casual approach. Exceptions are some of the CCT deities who appear as gently smiling "family members," kindly aunts or grandparents, for example. But even they often have unusual skin tones, suggesting that these are not mere mortals.

Some deities are recognizable, at least by association, because of the groupings in which they appear. Most important in this respect is the triad formation, generally depicting a main central figure flanked by two slightly smaller figures. Depending on the temple, these may depict any of several of the triadic variations mentioned above. Many temples install subordinate deities and semi-divine powers on side altars or in small rooms of their own along the inner perimeter of the main courtyard. Each deity has his or her distinguishing characteristics, but one generally finds fewer clear iconographic clues here than in Hindu or Buddhist art. For example, several deities may sport the same skin tones and facial expression and even carry very similar symbols. It is therefore sometimes impossible to discern the individual identities of the characters without knowing in advance to whom a given temple is dedicated.

67. What is the symbolism of the *trigrams* and their various permutations called *hexagrams*? Are there any other common *Chinese religious symbols?*

Trigrams are sets of three vertically stacked horizontal lines made up of every possible combination of broken (– –) and solid (—) lines. Solid lines stand for the solar male Yang, high, bright, active, and dry. Broken lines stand for the earthy and lunar female Yin, which is dark, moist, mysterious, and associated with valleys. Combinations of Yin and Yang in varying proportions give rise to the eight essential elements in creation. Traditional presentations usually arrange the eight trigrams as an octagon at whose center stands the *taiji* symbol for perfect Yin-Yang harmony. Each trigram is arrayed so as to face its opposite in the set. So, for example, if you held a compass before you with north pointing up, Heaven's three solid lines would stand across from Earth's three broken lines at what would be north and south. At due "east" stands Water, with a solid line between a pair of broken lines, across from Fire, with its broken line sandwiched between solids in the west. At northwest, Lake's broken-solid-solid (reading from top to bottom) stands opposite Mountain's solid-broken-broken. And in the northeast, Wind's solid-solid-broken balances off Thunder's broken-broken-solid. Take the eight trigrams and arrange them in all possible permutations by stacking one trigram atop another and you get sixty-four hexagrams. Pile Heaven upon Heaven and the result is called the "creative principle." Add Earth to Earth and you get the "passive principle." Earth over Heaven yields "peace," while Heaven over Earth means "stagnation." The single most important source for interpreting these arcane indicators is a classic work called the *Yijing,* the *Classic of Change.* Tossing and rearranging a set of fifty sticks and then reading them as hexagrams with the help of that text remains a widely popular form of divination.

Ancient lore associates fundamental features of Chinese cosmology with specific symbols. It all goes back to the "Chinese Adam," Pan Gu. In his task of imposing order on primal chaos, Pan Gu enlisted the help of five cosmic assistants: Azure Dragon, White Tiger, Phoenix, Tortoise, and Unicorn. Pan Gu assigned to each of the first four a quarter of the universe. Azure Dragon governed the East, associated with spring, new life, benevolence, and protection. White Tiger ruled the autumnal West, symbol of maturity and a life well-spent, all made possible by good government and courage. Phoenix, the ultimate solar bird, presided over the summery South with the kindly warmth and joy that arises in a world at peace. Hard-shelled and indomitable, the ageless Tortoise faced the unforgiving, wintry North. Wandering freely among them all, the rare and delicate Unicorn was commissioned to appear wherever and whenever benevolence and justice reigned on earth. It is not surprising that all five of these wondrous beings retain their appeal to the popular imagination and remain essentials of the religious symbolic repertoire.

Finally, a cluster of items associated loosely with Daoism is called the "Eight Daoist Emblems." Each represents one of the Eight Immortals, a group of human beings who attained immortality in various ways. They appear often as decorative motifs on all kinds of objects. The emblems are a fan, a sword, a gourd, castanets, a flower basket, a bamboo drum, a flute, and a lotus flower. This is one of several sets of eight motifs popular in Chinese art and, along with the Eight Buddhist Emblems, one that still carries specifically religious resonances.

68. What kinds of *ritual objects* are important in Chinese and Japanese traditions?

Confucianism/CIT: When Confucius was young, he was particularly intrigued by the classic bronze vessels his ancestors had used for centuries in honoring Heaven. Most of these vessels held materials to be offered. The principal forms developed in connection with the particular types of material. A vase called the *yu* was to hold sacrificial wine; a jug called *zhue* poured libations; and a beaker called *gu* may have been for sharing a communion-like drink. A *ding* was a bowl for ritual foods such as cereal grains or fruit. Some items were apparently designed in particularly symbolic shapes, such as the "hill-shaped" censer whose form recalled the Five Sacred Mountains. Some bronzes bear abstract representations of the four directional creatures: the black tortoise of the wintry north, the green dragon of the vernal east, the scarlet bird of the summery south, and the white tiger of the autumnal west. Inscriptions dedicating an object to a father, for example, or expressing the hope that sons and grandsons would use the vessel for "ten thousand years" suggest that they were commonly used in ancestor veneration rituals. Even today, copies of those antique objects adorn the altars in Confucian temples and are part of the relatively infrequent offerings held there. Many of the sacred vessels were buried in tombs or even thrown into riverbeds during invasions to prevent them from falling into the hands of barbarians. Nearly every large museum has good examples in its Asian collections, and they are well worth a visit.

Daoism: Specific lists of objects vary somewhat among the different schools and sects. Here are the most important ritual devices of the Celestial Masters school. First and foremost are the ubiquitous talismans that consist of a written magical formula or mantra symbolizing a contract between the deities and human beings engaging in a ritual exchange. Only a qualified ritual specialist may execute a talisman, which usually includes a Chinese character as well as other visual symbols appropriate to a particular spiritual purpose. Possessors of talismans generally think of them as guarantees of divine aid. People wear them or hang them in home or office as protective devices. The "Precious Sword of the Seven Stars," symbolizing the Big Dipper, appears often in blessings and exorcisms, whether for individuals or as part of Cosmic Renewal observances. As a symbolic purification of the cardinal directions, ritualists sip from a copper bowl and blow a spray through closed lips. Stone seals of various kinds allow the ritualist to make official documents such as talismans. Priests hold a stiff tablet, as if reading from a book. In exorcism rituals, Black Hats use the sword along with handbells, while Red Turbans use a horn and a whip.

Shinto: Shinto tradition refers to all of its "ritual furniture and utensils" with the term *saikigu.* It includes several items used on every altar during offering ceremonies. The priest carries the offerings *(heihaku)* and gifts of food *(shinsen)* on a tray *(sambo),* which he sets upon an eight-legged table *(hassokuan)* made of a reddish cypress wood *(hinoki,* "fire tree"). Priestly staff remove these objects after worship ends. Objects used regularly in nearly all rituals include several items that ritual specialists wave over those to whom they are ministering. Branches of the *sakaki* (combining characters for "tree" and *"kami")* provide a splash of greenery and association with living nature. A wand used for purification, either in place of or in conjunction with the *sakaki* branch, is called *haraigushi*—a thick cluster of white paper streamers attached to a long stick. Another stick with a set of zigzag-cut white (and sometimes colored) paper symbolizes *kami* presence in the holy place. All three objects are mounted on stands and displayed when not in use by one of the priests or a *miko. Miko* also use a set of five bells *(suzu)* for their sacred dances.

Several larger implements play a central role in the great public festivals called *matsuri.* Most important is the portable shrine called the *mikoshi.* Celebrants carry this miniature, but still often very heavy, four-sided model of a shrine sanctuary in procession, shouldering long beams that hold the shrine aloft. Larger *mikoshi* can weigh up to several tons and require a large crew of strong bearers. In some places, large wagons called *yatai* and *dashi* rumble through the streets on massive wheels, carrying groups of musicians and revelers. Built like mobile shrines, the hefty wooden wagons range in height from just over thirty feet to about sixty-five feet.

69. How important is *music* in the Chinese and Japanese traditions?

Confucianism/CIT: Celebrations like that of Confucius's birthday are filled with the sound of music. Confucius always insisted that training in both music appreciation and instrumental proficiency were essential ingredients in a proper education. Many Confucian temples keep the principal musical instruments on display in the main memorial hall flanking the tablet of Confucius. Important stringed instruments include plucked cousins of the Japanese *koto* called the *jin* and *se,* which are not typically found in Daoist instrumental ensembles. Percussion pieces include a variety of bells, both individual large ones and sets of tuned smaller ones, and similar sets of metal chimes. Wind instruments include multi-tube flutes, similar to the European Pan flute, as well as wooden transverse flutes.

A category of decorative motifs called the "Eight Musical Instruments" appear on all sorts of fine wares, suggesting the importance of music in Chinese tradition. The eight instruments include the musical stone, a large bell, a lute, a flute, a metal percussion instrument, a drum, a reed organ, and an ocarina. The CIT rituals always included large musical ensembles that played during lengthy segments of the ceremonies, especially for the entrance and exit of the emperor and while the royal subjects were paying homage to the sovereign.

Daoism/CCT: Music has been an essential ingredient in virtually all indigenous Chinese religious ritual for millennia. Students of Daoist masters are expected to begin their formal training by becoming accomplished in the use of a full range of string, wind, and percussion instruments. These ancient devices include not only the mysterious booming gongs and bowed or plucked strings many readers may already associate with Asian music, but the less well-known woodwinds whose high reedy voices produce an almost eerie effect. Daoist ritual music has been related to imperial court music and, somewhat more recently, to Chinese opera.

Ritual music aims at stirring feelings uniquely appropriate to the occasion. In this respect, Daoist ritual music has much in common with the music that is an essential ingredient in many Shinto ceremonies in Japan. Two percussion instruments used to keep time for chanting and recitation of scripture are virtually identical to those used for the same purpose in Buddhist ritual all over Asia. For large-scale chanting on especially solemn occasions, an ensemble of four or more instruments of various types provides accompaniment. Percussion instruments along with other wind and string instruments back up the lead played on oboe-like woodwinds, lutes, and bowed strings. When a single master recites a sacred text, a solo instrument is generally the only accompaniment.

Shinto: Not long ago, I had the rare privilege of experiencing a performance of *gagaku,* "refined music," by the musicians of the Suwa Shrine in Japan's Nagano prefecture. *Gagaku* is ancient courtly music originating in China as early as the Han dynasty and cultivated by the Japanese in Heian imperial circles. Often associated with dance, the fourteen-person instrumental ensemble consists of percussions and reeds. But it also includes the long, Hawaiian-guitar-like plucked string called the *so,* cousin of the larger *koto,* identifiable by its frequent use of the technique of note-bending. A plucked string called the *biwa* is also part of the ensemble. Woodwinds are the "three reeds" *(sankan),* piccolo-like six- and nine-hole flutes, a primitive oboe-like woodwind that produces a sharp, edgy sound, and a cluster of seventeen bamboo pipes called the *sho* that is in fact a tiny pipe organ for the mouth. Slow, stately rhythms beat out by the percussions underlie the haunting, almost plaintive sounds of the high-pitched reeds.

Only the rarest of sounds can communicate aptly the sense of solemnity and perfect "otherness" of the deities the music addresses in Shinto shrines, and these instruments do just that. Most non-Japanese who encounter music identified as Japanese are likely to associate that musical tradition with the sound of plucked strings, such as the *koto* and *shamisen.* In Shinto shrine ritual, however, stringed instruments do not play the major role they play in Chinese ritual. Percussion and woodwinds make up the bulk of the typical ceremonial ensemble. Percussion instruments include the massive *taiko,* a large barrel with two skin heads that sits sideways on an elevated stand just inside the outer ritual hall of larger shrines. A shrine ritualist, often one of the *miko* ("deaconesses"), announces the beginning of ceremonies by a pulse-pounding crescendo-decrescendo on the great drum. Various smaller drums keep time for dances.

70. Is *dance* also a significant ingredient in these traditions?

Confucianism/CIT: Once a central feature of many rituals in China, Confucian dance has been preserved as an art form only in Korea. During the semi-annual gathering to honor the spirits of Confucius and the sages at the Confucian University, and at the annual gathering to honor the kings of the Yi dynasty at the Royal Ancestral Shrine, dancers perform elaborate routines. Originally Confucian dance was limited to male performers. Both military and non-military forms of dance make up the repertoire. Dancers gesture with the long pheasant feathers and small flute they carry. Elaborate ritual movement was formerly integral to virtually all the major ceremonies of the CIT. Whether in the courtyards of the Forbidden City or around the altars of the Temple of Heaven and other sacred imperial sites, intricately choreographed scripts called for dance on a grand scale.

Daoism: During the Cosmic Renewal Festival, for example, the principal ritual specialist performs a dance of shamanic origin called the Steps of Yu. The dancer traces out the outline of the Big

Dipper to commune with the god of the Pole Star. He ascends symbolically into the heavens to visit the Three Pure Ones. Some dances engage the assembled community of worshipers, as when all gathered celebrate the new light by circumambulating the altar. Another dance functions as an offertory procession in which worshipers bring gifts to the ritual leaders who in turn present them to the gods.

Shinto: *Bugaku,* "refined dance" in 160 different styles, is often performed to the accompaniment of a *gagaku* ensemble and sometimes occurs in Buddhist temples as well as Shinto shrines. It is somewhat more formal and classical than *kagura,* a uniquely Shinto form of liturgical dance with musical accompaniment. The name *kagura* apparently derives from a term that means "temporary abode of the *kami,*" a place on earth to which worshipers summon the deities. *Kagura* has its mythic roots in the dance of the Terrible Female of Heaven that lured the sun goddess to emerge from her cave. Unlike the more staid classical version danced for the emperor on December's full-moon night, shrine (or village) *kagura* now reenacts often raucous scenes from mythological narratives.

Several of the great shrines, such as those of Izumo, Kasuga, and Ise, are known for their long-standing traditions of *kagura* performance. Some shrines have structures dedicated to *kagura,* but many still stage the dance in the large open space in front of the *haiden. Bon odori* is a popular form of folk dancing done at festivals on shrine grounds. Celebrants dance around a large raised scaffold-like platform on which drummers and other musicians perch to play their popular *hayashi*-style music. Perhaps the best known of Shinto-related dances is the Dragon Dance often associated with festival parades. In shrine dances, the dragon begins by bowing to the *kami* and the chief priest before writhing its way across the sacred precincts. The ancient Japanese theater form called *No* also has roots in the reenactment of Shinto myths.

SEVEN:

INTERNAL DIVERSITY AND EXTERNAL RELATIONS

71. Have there been any sub-communities or *denominations within Confucianism?*

An early historian of Confucian tradition, Liu Xiang (77–6 B.C.E.), claimed that by his time the Confucians had divided into one hundred and three schools of thought, each defined by its distinctive manner of interpreting the essential texts. Whether that was literally the case or not, it is clear there were a number of groups representing notably diverse views and methods. Here are some brief hints at how several of those schools developed.

Mozi (468–390 B.C.E.) started out as a Confucian but went his own way, opting for a less stratified, more egalitarian model of society. Some have characterized Mozi as a pragmatist because he insisted that observable improvement in the welfare of the populace was the ultimate criterion of good public policy. Confucius, he argued, put too much emphasis on ritual and filial devotion and too little on measurably advancing civilization. Mozi taught the importance of striving for a society united by a mutual love that amounted to a form of enlightened self-interest. His school flourished for just over a century, but it offers a glimpse at one of several credible critiques of the classical Confucian approach. Another dissenting voice of Mozi's era was that of the Legalists *(Fajia)*. They took Mozi's critique several steps further from Confucius's global confidence that the mere example of virtuous leadership could bring about a moral conversion in society. Governance, they argued, required clear and comprehensive legislation that capitalized on people's fear of punishment and hope of reward. Confucius and Mozi clearly had greater faith in human perfectibility and in a reservoir of good will at the heart of humankind.

During the Song (960–1279) and later dynasties, several important schools developed within the larger phenomenon called Neo-Confucianism. The two main branches became known as the

School of Principle and the School of Mind, according to their respective theoretical points of departure. The School of Principle (Lixue) was also called the Cheng Zhu school, combining the first names of the men it claims as its founders, Cheng Yi (1033–1107), and his brother Cheng Hao (1032–1085), and the later Zhuxi (1130–1200). The brothers Cheng developed a sophisticated theory in which "principle" *(li)* meant, not the classical Confucian rites and canons of social propriety, but an unchanging universal law inherent in all nature. Zhuxi further refined that concept of principle, defining it as the Great Ultimate from which all forces in nature emerge. In what one might call a variety of "process theology," Zhuxi argued that the path to ethical development was "the investigation of things." The other major branch of neo-Confucian thinking was known as the School of Mind (Xinxue). Wang Yangming (1472–1529) was one of the school's leading lights. Principle, he argued, was not merely a transcendent and inaccessible cosmic force, but was one with the human mind. He taught that one could cultivate good conduct through "reverent seriousness," a type of meditative discipline through which one could realize the unity of mind and principle.

72. Have there been any important sub-communities or *denominations within Daoism?*

Dozens of schools and sects have arisen over the long history of religious Daoism. Here are a few of the more important ones. The Great Purity school (Shangqing), also known as Mount Mao (Mao Shan) Daoism, developed during the late fourth century. The Shangqing claims as its central revelation a set of scriptural texts in over thirty volumes. Almost contemporary in origin with that school is another called the Lingbao, which also claims a distinctive scriptural revelation based in part on the Shangqing scripture. Heavenly Mind (Tianxin) Daoism, emphasizing the importance of exorcism and based also on its own scriptural revelation, began in the late tenth century. The Divine Highest Heaven

(Shen Xiao) school, dating from the twelfth century, is best known for its talismans of legendary potency and its elucidation of correspondences between the microcosm of the body and the macrocosm of the universe. Great Oneness (Taiyi) Daoism, also from the twelfth century, was a celibate monastic school important for its integration of Confucian and Buddhist elements. Though none of these schools remains active today, all have made significant historical contributions to the large and complex reality called Daoism.

Daoism's Celestial Masters school (Tianshi Dao, also called Zhengyi, "Correct One") stands out as the original institutional expression of religious Daoism and one of several early attempts to establish theocratic communities. It was originally known as the Five Bushels of Rice school, after the "dues" expected of members. Founded by Zhang Daoling (34–156 C.E.) in about 142, the sect focused initially on physical, moral, and spiritual healing through ritual confession of faults and exorcism. Regular rituals included recitation from the *Daodejing* and communal meals, with special feasts three times annually to acknowledge the three celestial bureaucracies overseeing heaven, earth, and water.

Over the centuries the Celestial Masters school has worked to prevent the popularization of religious rituals by attempting to maintain standards in the training of ritual specialists. Two main divisions, the southern and northern schools, developed more or less independently and then merged around the fourteenth century. After losing ground to various other schools for many centuries, the school has risen to prominence in modern times and now generally dominates the formal practice of Daoism and its rituals. The school is represented officially by the sixty-third Master who lives in exile in Taiwan.

Founded by Wang Zhe (c. 1123–1170, also called Wang Chongyang), the Perfect Realization (Chuanzhen) school is among the most important Daoist monastic orders. According to legend, Wang Zhe received new revelations from one of the Eight Immortals, Lu Dongbin. A central feature in the order's discipline was ascetical self-denial, including meditative practices designed to maximize Yang energy and minimize Yin. The founder evidently insisted on the importance of studying the teachings of Buddhism and Confucianism along with those of Daoism, but focused on the characteristically Daoist spiritual goal of immortality. Of its several branches, the Longmen ("Dragon Gate") is perhaps the most influential. Like religious orders in some other major traditions, the Perfect Realization order has historically been socially active and responsible for preserving much traditional Chinese religious culture in times of turmoil. For example, in 1192 it published a major edition of the Daoist scriptural canon and it has done extensive refugee relief work. From the White Cloud monastery in Beijing, the Longmen branch of the order continues its work today.

73. Are there any sub-communities or *denominations within Shinto?* Have "orthodoxy" and "heresy" been significant Shinto concepts?

Numerous varieties and schools of Shinto have come and gone over the past thirteen hundred years. Thirteen principal sects collectively comprise what is generally referred to as "sectarian" or "sect" (Kyoha) Shinto. Arising over the centuries and officially recognized in the early twentieth century, the thirteen cluster around several themes or emphases. First, two groups that emphasize purification are known as Misogikyo and Shinshukyo (-*kyo* means teaching or school). An ascetical "mountain" sect called Shugendo began as early as the Nara period (710–784), and small affiliated groups remain active today. Fusokyo, Jikkokyo, and Ontakekyo are today called "mountain sects" because they center around cults of two sacred mountains, Fuji and Ontake. They restructured along distinctively Shinto lines the teachings of several earlier ascetically oriented Shugendo groups.

Beginning during the middle ages, several *schools* arose under the patronage of important members of powerful clans. Now identified by the names of those families or of the schools' individual founders, the larger groups are Urabe (also known by the later family name of Yoshida, and Yuiitsu ["unification"] Shinto), Watarai (also called Ise Shinto), and the Confucian-oriented school of Yoshikawa. Three more recent *sects* have focused on faith healing: Kurozumikyo, Tenrikyo, and Konkokyo all trace their origins to a founding figure. Two sects called Shinto Shuseiha and Shinto Taiseikyo have emphasized Confucian elements and have blended features of the purification and mountain sects as well.

Several other *schools* are identified by terms that suggest their principal teaching or emphases. For example, a seventeenth century school called Suiga ("Bestowal of Blessings") Shinto laid groundwork for the growth of "National Learning." Sanno Ichijitsu blended Shinto themes with esoteric teachings of Tendai Buddhism in the seventeenth century, focusing on the divine manifestation of a "mountain king" *(sanno)*. Finally among the "thirteen" come the most recent groups, whose mission has been to renew Shinto tradition. They are Izumo Oyashirokyo, Shinrikyo, and Shinto Taikyo. The latter is an umbrella organization that was largely responsible for the official recognition of the thirteen. From these sects dozens of smaller movements have arisen in recent times.

Minkan Shinko is a general designation for a host of developments called "folk" religious beliefs and practices, incorporating elements of Shinto as well as other traditions. Especially since the late nineteenth century, Japanese governments have promulgated various types of legislation aimed at keeping track of the many religious groups that have occasionally leveled severe criticism at the imperial form of governance. In addition, several of Japan's so-called "new religions" have developed out of mainstream Shinto within the past two centuries or so. Some traditionally minded Japanese may be inclined to regard them with suspicion, possibly even labeling them as dangerous "cults." Sociologically speaking, a number of these groups qualify as schismatic, that is "splinter" groups, in that they have deliberately parted company with ancient Shinto tradition. Some scholars suggest that Shinto authorities coined terms such as "The Emperor's Way" *(kodo)* and "The *Kami*-ordained Way" *(kannagara no michi)* to distinguish a type of Shinto "orthodoxy" from a host of less correct popular and folk beliefs. But since the concept of "orthodoxy" has been far less important for Shinto tradition than it has for, say, some Christian or Muslim communities, the notion of "heresy" is largely irrelevant here.

74. Is the phenomenon of *conversion into the traditions* of China and Japan important?

Confucianism: Confucian tradition has been so deeply identified with Chinese culture that the notion of "converting" into the tradition is virtually meaningless. That is not to say that individuals have not been so highly attracted to the teachings of the tradition that they have espoused it as a philosophy of life. But so much of Confucianism is inseparable from such practices as ancestor veneration and other culturally rooted behavior that the likelihood of conversion is very small. In addition, over the centuries most people one might identify as Confucian have more than likely been associated with other religious traditions as well, such as Daoism, CCT, or Buddhism. In Chinese religious history, and Japanese too, the more or less tidy distinctions many Europeans and Americans are used to making between religious communities simply have not been applicable.

Daoism: In relatively recent times, Daoism has enjoyed something of a renaissance in mainland China and has attracted increasing interest among people outside of China. A quick scan of Internet sites affords a fair impression of contemporary Euro-American interpretations of the ancient Chinese tradition. Many non-Chinese who are attracted to Daoism gravitate toward the philosophical rather than to the theistic or religious elements. Some proponents of "New Age" beliefs have adopted the use of Daoist divinatory techniques, especially the interpretation of the hexagrams by consulting the *Yijing*. But on the whole, non-Chinese who express an active interest in Daoism do not "convert" into the tradition the way one would when becoming, say, a Muslim or a Christian. Since Daoism is so intertwined with an integrated worldview that is profoundly Chinese, it is almost a contradiction in terms to talk of "becoming a Daoist." Rare individuals have, however, so thoroughly entered into Daoism as to become spiritual masters.

Shinto: Since Shinto is so intimately identified with being Japanese, the concept of conversion is largely irrelevant. That does not mean that no non-Japanese has ever deliberately chosen to become a practitioner of Shinto, but such instances are very rare. The case of Judaism offers a rough parallel. Many consider membership in Judaism a matter of ethnicity, but some Jewish congregations nevertheless welcome converts into their faith community. Several Jewish congregations have developed formal initiatory rites for ethnically non-Jewish individuals, but Shinto tradition apparently does not have such rites for non-Japanese who wish to practice and profess the Shinto tradition. One difference here is that membership in Judaism presupposes assent to certain basic creedal affirmations whereas Shinto does not.

75. Have the Chinese and Japanese religious traditions typically sent out *missionaries* to convert others?

Confucianism: Confucius was genuinely convinced that his ethical views and integrated approach to just government under the dominion of Heaven had much to recommend them. He himself was a zealous advocate and spent much of his life trying to "convert" others to his interpretation of the human condition. When at length the Confucian system took hold as the theory behind the practice of imperial administration, the bureaucratic structure itself became the mechanism that spread Confucian thinking far and wide. Diplomatic relations with other lands became a network for the export of the Confucian way. But neither Confucius nor his most influential disciples were populists. Instead of preaching to the masses as missionary movements typically do, Confucians have espoused a "trickle-down" theory. Convince the leaders and they in turn will spread the word to their subjects. Persuade those in authority to model the good society. Given appropriate official sanctions and incentives, the people will see the benefit of establishing proper relationships at every level.

Daoism/CCT: Daoism has not generally been a mission-oriented tradition. There have been periods in the history of China during which Daoist authorities have made it clear that life would be more difficult for non-Daoists. A number of Chinese emperors espoused Daoism as the official state creed, in effect, and attempted to cleanse the realm of Buddhists. And there have been times when Daoists have been in serious competition with Confucians. But, on the whole, systematic missionary activity is not the essential ingredient in Daoism that it has been in Islam, Buddhism, and Christianity. When Daoism and CCT have spread they have done so largely as a result of migration of Chinese merchant families.

Shinto: Shinto has been so closely identified with Japanese culture as to be virtually inseparable from it. A desire to spread Shinto with missionary zeal would make about as much sense as wishing one could turn non-Japanese persons into Japanese. It is as unnecessary as it is impossible. Even the most devoted and active practitioners of Shinto do not generally feel themselves called to spread the tradition. At the heart of Shinto is a primordial wisdom that cannot be taught or spread by decree. It is as natural as breathing. Of course, everyone is better off breathing, but it's not something one can teach. Since the tradition is passed on organically, so to speak, and inherited as a family and national treasure, practitioners do not think of it as something necessary for the betterment—or salvation—of humanity. At the same time, active members of local Shinto communities remain hospitable to a fault. Arrive at a shrine during a festival and, however much you may stand out from the crowd, chances are good that someone will invite you to participate in the celebration.

76. Do people ever decide they want to *depart from* Daoism/CCT or Shinto?

Daoism/CCT: Membership in Daoism and CCT has rarely, if ever, been a matter of exclusive allegiance. Members of some major religious traditions, such as Islam, Christianity, Judaism, and, to a lesser degree, Hinduism, typically regard "belonging" as a kind of all-or-nothing affair. Either you're in or you're out. Disagree with major tenets of the tradition, or neglect consistently and willfully to fulfill the minimum ritual and ethical requirements of the faith community and your membership is in question—or has lapsed altogether. Religiously involved Chinese generally do not think about membership in those terms. Belonging is deeply rooted in national and local culture, integral to the very fabric of society. Individuals who drift away from regular religious practice have not necessarily "left," so long as they have not entirely cut themselves off from family and social connections. Other family members might express regret that sons or daughters no longer find the traditional ways helpful and choose to delete that part of their heritage from their self-identities. And many today sense the gradual diminishment of traditional values and practices precisely because of this sort of attrition. But Chinese, whether Daoist or CCT, generally do not think in terms of "leaving the faith" unless they do so with the intention of converting to a missionary faith, such as Christianity. In those cases, people do talk of leaving behind unacceptable beliefs and practices.

Shinto: Membership in traditions so closely identified with ethnicity as Shinto has a great deal to do with trends in society generally. That is of course true of most religious traditions, but here there are several features worth noting. Japanese ethnicity does not imply adherence to Shinto beliefs and practices any more than Jewish ancestry implies that an individual actively participates in Judaic religious traditions. Shinto is integral to the fabric of Japanese life. Large numbers of Japan's present population do not engage in regular Shinto rituals at all, and many others are very selective as to their involvement. But that does not imply a deliberate choice to reject the ancient traditions as such. It does, however, underscore the impact of cultural and social change on all things traditional. Shinto tradition calls people to unhurried, careful attentiveness to the mysterious details of life. In a fast-paced, often tumultuous world, the drumbeat of change can easily drown out the sound of the drums that announce the beginning of a sacred ritual.

77. How would you sum up *Confucianism's historical relationships* to other traditions?

Confucianism's most important and enduring inter-religious relations have been with Buddhism and Daoism. There have been periods during which Confucians have had more or less cordial dealings with representatives of the other two "ways" of China. But since so much has often been at stake, especially in terms of imperial patronage, Confucian scholars have frequently leveled serious criticisms at Daoist and Buddhist views. For example, Confucians have sometimes faulted Buddhism for being too other-worldly, too disconnected from the ordinary problems and needs of regular people. Confucians have generally interpreted the Buddhist ideal of celibate monastic life as an abdication of filial devotion and the responsibility to perpetuate the family lineage.

Daoists, on the other hand, have characteristically struck Confucians as frankly naive in their conviction that, if left to themselves, people will naturally follow an exemplary leader. Daoism's emphasis on doing things nature's way leaves society too vulnerable to simple lawlessness. In addition, the Confucian tradition's strong emphasis on education has appeared to many to be irreconcilable with Daoism's more "organic" and seemingly anti-intellectual approach to learning. When the Confucian tradition began to come into prominence during Japan's Tokugawa era, it found an increasingly hostile official response from representatives of Shinto. Confucianism, Shinto authorities argued, was a non-Japanese influence and therefore undesirable. By that time, however, Confucius had already made an indelible impression on Japanese society.

78. How would you describe *Daoism's relationships* to other traditions?

By the beginning of the first millennium, philosophically minded Daoists had rubbed elbows for several centuries with proponents of a cultural and ethical system often identified as Confucian. Together, the Confucians and the Daoists were increasingly important elements of a larger cultural matrix. "Religion," for which they had as yet no specific term, was a blend of ancient divinatory rites, ancestor veneration, exorcism, and offerings meant to secure blessings and protection from "Heaven" and several other fairly generic and non-personal divine powers. Religious Daoism evolved during the period when Buddhism was taking root in China. It was not until Chinese Buddhism was several centuries old that Chinese thinkers began to talk of "three ways" of being both Chinese and religious. It is as though the Chinese people had not thought of their ancient traditions as anything but "the way things are," rather like the air they breathed, until an imported variety of thinking and acting called the Way of the Buddha entered the scene.

Buddhist-Daoist relations have had a checkered history. At first many Daoists regarded Buddhism as a new Daoist school or sect, thanks to Buddhist efforts at translating key concepts into terms Daoists would understand. Before long, full-scale hostility developed when Daoists began to think of the missionary-minded Buddhists as a threat. Confucians often sided with Daoists in condemning Buddhism as "un-Chinese." Periods of persecution of Buddhists alternated with rich interchange and mutual influence. Since the 1800s Daoist-Buddhist relations have been much more stable and peaceful, so that many Chinese now perceive few or no important distinctions or barriers between the two traditions. CCT has been a kind of meeting ground. As for Daoist-Confucian relations, there has been an off-and-on rivalry for imperial patron-age. The two traditions share a great deal in the way of broad doc-trinal and cultural themes, such as the so-called Yin/Yang worldview and ancestor veneration. During the Confucian revival of the twelfth and thirteenth centuries, the development known as Neo-Confucianism, there was renewed positive interaction and mutual exchange of ideas. Nowadays, relations continue on a generally cordial basis but without much substantial discussion of core beliefs.

79. What issues have characterized *Shinto's relationships* to other traditions?

Shinto has had important connections especially to Buddhism and Confucianism, and secondarily to the Christianity that mission-aries brought to Japan in the early modern period. During much of medieval and early modern times, Shinto and Buddhist leaders and teachers worked at articulating points of theological cooperation between various schools of thought in the two traditions. That ongoing interaction resulted in the various types of Ryobu, or Two-sided, Shinto as well as other syncretistic denominations and sects. Such cooperation continued until the thirteenth and fourteenth cen-turies, when some Shinto thinkers developed systems in which Shinto stood at the top of a theological mountain.

By the seventeenth century, the "National Learning" move-ment began to offer a fully articulated interpretation of Buddhist-Shinto relations. Scholars suggested that the major figures of the Buddhist pantheon were nothing more than local forms of the *kami* and that the emperor had descended directly from the Sun goddess, Amaterasu. Confucianism had by that time made its presence felt more vigorously than ever through its impact on courtly life and administration of the Tokugawa shogunate (1600–1867). Confucian scholars and bureaucrats also con-tributed significantly to the Meiji Restoration in 1868. But the more closely Shinto theology came to be identified with the

Japanese throne, the more it developed into a national ideology with little room for systems of belief considered non-Japanese—Buddhism and Confucianism, first and foremost, but now missionary Christianity as well. Contemporary Shinto has once again become more open to interaction with other traditions, and Shinto leaders take it for granted that many who worship at shrines also maintain other religious affiliations. For many Japanese, the *Kami* Way is not a separate system of religious beliefs. It is simply what all religious persons believe underneath all their otherwise distinctive doctrines. Shinto is therefore nothing less than the very essence of acknowledging the divine in the world.

EIGHT:

WOMEN, FAMILY, AND SOCIETY

80. What *gender-related issues* have been important in these traditions? Have women exercised religious *leadership and authority?*

Confucianism/CIT: Confucian tradition emphasized social order, and that called for clearly delineated gender functions. Given the conviction that only a patriarchal structure could guarantee social order, what many people today call "social equality" was simply not included in the Confucian lexicon. Confucian teaching envisioned male-female relationships according to a political model. First and foremost among questions of gender were those relating to family structure and roles. But whether within the family or in society at large, women and younger people generally shared the expectation of dutiful obedience. Women remained in the home to serve the family, which sometimes brought as many as four generations together in one household. Widows were typically expected not to remarry. When a wife produced no son, a husband could marry one or more secondary wives in the hope of securing a male heir. A telling fact is that no women are numbered among the great sages and scholars memorialized in Confucian temples. In the imperial household, there were sometimes several empresses and many royal concubines. An empress remained out of view for the most part, participating in a few affairs of state annually. Eunuchs looked after the harem, strictly organizing the lives of all the women in the imperial household.

Confucian tradition is staunchly patriarchal. Long-standing practice all over Asia, as a result of Confucian influence, has until only recently expected women to obey father before marriage, husband during marriage, and oldest son when her husband dies. Education under classical Confucian direction was limited to males. That is no longer the case in societies that still acknowledge, however indirectly, their Confucian heritage. As for the

CIT, a number of empresses and princesses came to prominence over the centuries, but here too the rule was male leadership. Empresses were generally in charge of the so-called inner court. Empress-mothers frequently had duties in matters of state and thus were often more active in the outside world. Women were never allowed in the main halls of the Forbidden City's outer court, except on the day a new empress married her emperor.

Daoism: One of the most famous libationers was a woman named Wei Huacun (251–334 C.E.). Her rank as libationer apparently indicates that she originally belonged to the Celestial Masters school. Some regard her as a foundational figure in the Shangqing (Great Purity) school. She is perhaps most famous for having appeared posthumously on many nights over a six-year period to reveal to a certain Yang Xi the sacred texts of the Shangqing sect. Those texts consist mainly of liturgical ritual. Throughout its long history, the Celestial Masters school has allowed women into the lower rungs of its ritual hierarchy, up to but not including that of Celestial Master itself. Another school, called "Pure Rarity" (Qingwei), is said to have been founded by a woman named Zushu in the early tenth century. Centered around a thunder deity, the sect blended elements from the Lingbao, Shangqing, and Celestial Masters schools. There have been many women priestesses over the centuries, and a celibate community of women maintains a temple in Kaoshung, Taiwan.

Hagiographical sources are extant on a number of holy women of ancient times. These sources make it clear that women who preferred to pursue the spiritual life rather than devote themselves to family risked almost certain disapproval. Even so, it seems that some women were associated with religious orders. Sun Buer (1119–1182) and her husband were both ritual specialists in the Perfect Realization order, and she founded a new division of the school dedicated to the religious education of women. A selection of her writings in translation is available in Thomas Cleary's *Immortal Sisters: Secret Teachings of Taoist Women.* A sect associated especially with the Red Turbans is popularly called San Nai, "Three Ladies," evidently so named to honor a trio of priestesses about whom little else is known. As has often been the case in other religious traditions, many Chinese women have found possibilities for active leadership and ministry more often outside the institutional structures than within.

Shinto: Shinto priests (and priestesses) have almost always been married people with families. Ongoing social taboo still prohibits menstruating women from participating as official ministers in ritual activities. Contemporary custom, however, has in all likelihood loosened such restrictions. It is safe to say that in general women have historically had greater direct participation in many Shinto shrine rituals than they do presently. Only unmarried young women are eligible for the office of *miko* in shrines, and typically have access to the positions hereditarily, as a result of their families' priestly traditions.

Even after imperial decrees reduced women's roles in shrine life, giving precedence to a male priesthood, women continued to fill some key positions. Well into the sixteenth century, for example, women functioned as priestesses in some shrines. The last of the priestesses is a young woman serving the Suwa Shrine in Nagasaki. Women have long acted as spirit mediums consulted by many a priest over the centuries, as well as by individual worshipers. Restrictive legislation arising from the Meiji Restoration in 1868 dramatically curtailed women's official participation in shrine staff ministries. Only at the Ise Grand Shrine, sacred to the sun goddess Amaterasu, does a woman currently hold the position of high priestess. During the Second World War, many women took over priestly functions when their husbands departed for military service. In ancient times shamanesses were very important in Shinto circles. Today the shrine maidens, *miko,* may represent a vestige of that ritual specialization of long ago.

Blind female shamans called *itako* still ply their trade in various parts of Japan. Strict asceticism marks the apprenticeship of young blind girls to older teachers. After lengthy training the aspirant marries a *kami* symbolically to secure spiritual power and protection. Shamanesses perform the service of connecting with the *kami* world, sometimes functioning as spirit mediums. Some of the so-called New Religions with Shinto roots give prominent roles to shamanesses. Ancient Shinto tradition associates certain forms of spirit possession with shamanesses, explaining their extraordinary powers in unusual circumstances. Newer sects such as Tenrikyo acknowledge that male or female shamans experience a *"kami* descent" *(kami-gakari)* in which the deity takes over the human being totally.

81. Who are some important *female deities?*

Daoism/CCT: A legendary woman named Xiwangmu, also known as the Queen Mother of the West, figures prominently in some Daoist writings. She is a patroness of immortality, often depicted in the company of Jade Maidens, one carrying a fan and the other a bushel of the peaches of longevity. A goddess named Doumu (Mother of the Bushel of Stars, or Northern Dipper) functions in Daoism much the way Guanyin does in Buddhism, offering limitless compassion for the suffering. Another widely popular goddess in CCT is Mazu, sometimes called "Holy Heavenly Mother." She actually lived during the tenth century and was formally deified by several emperors during the twelfth and thirteenth centuries. Originally patroness of sailors and rescuer from storms, she soon became famous for a wider range of powers. Taiwan alone has several hundred Mazu temples, where she sits enthroned and crowned with a royal diadem befitting the Empress of Heaven. In some temples she is also called Great Auntie or Grandmother in keeping with the general conception of the deities as part of an all-embracing extended family.

Shinto: Amaterasu, the sun goddess, is the most important of the goddesses. Hundreds of shrines throughout Japan are dedicated to her. One of the most colorful goddesses is Ama no Uzume, the "terrible female of heaven," widely popular because of her identification with frivolity and dance. A *kami* described as

Altar in a family temple dedicated to the Empress of the West, known also as Mazu and by a variety of other names, in Honolulu. Many such altars hold more than one image of the central deity. Note the larger image in the background partially concealed by the drapery. (Thanks to Mrs. Au for showing the author around the temple.)

both masculine and feminine is Inari. Because of her association with the rice harvest, Inari is among the most important deities. Her messenger is the fox, and popular custom often refers to the fox itself as Inari. Bright reddish-orange or red *torii* gates, sometimes in great numbers, usually mark shrines dedicated to Inari.

A pair of goddesses associated with the war *kami* Hachiman sometimes appear in a sculptural triad with Hachiman. One is called Nakatsuhime, but the other remains to be identified. Seiryu Gongen was one of several goddesses adopted by Shinto in their role as protectors of Buddhist temples. Two other "imported" goddesses with Buddhist connections are Zenmyo Nyoshin and Byakukoshin. Stories tell of how a Korean monk fell in love with Zenmyo while he was studying in China. Byakuko was once an

Indian earth deity who became a Shinto *kami* through her association with powers of nature. Goddesses like Kumano Fusumi
Okami are often depicted round and full to suggest abundance.
The goddess Tamayorihime appears in a triad, flanked by two
other goddesses, once worshiped as the "three protectresses of
children." Tamayori was the daughter of Watatsumi no Kami,
kami of the oceans, and Japan's first emperor's mother.

Benten (also called Benzaiten) is a goddess of Indian origin.
Hindus know her as Sarasvati, consort of the god Brahma and
patroness of culture. She plays the Japanese lute (called the *biwa*),
as Sarasvati plays the veena, and devotees beseech her for protection and for gifts of eloquence and knowledge. Numerous female
kami have played important roles in Shinto life over the centuries,
and some were frequently depicted in human form, but only a few
remain significant in contemporary devotion.

82. Has *religiously sponsored education* played an important role?

Confucianism: No major religious tradition has placed
greater emphasis on education than Confucianism. That is not to
suggest that Confucian teaching reduces the truth to mere intellectual development. For Confucians, education goes far beyond
developing mental skills and acquiring information. It means cultivation of the whole person within the broadest possible perspective—humanism under Heaven. A number of very important
Confucian institutions of higher learning have made major contributions throughout Asia over the centuries. Perhaps even more
pervasive has been the Confucian influence in the development
and maintenance of China's imperial civil service system, the
educational system that produced and regulated the social class
called the Literati.

Daoism/CCT: People born into Chinese families with a long
history of associations with Daoism or CCT, or both, grow up
hearing about traditional beliefs. They participate, practically
from infancy, in family home, and perhaps also temple, rituals,

and almost certainly learn the ways of ancestor veneration. There has generally been no need for an educational network designed to preserve ancient beliefs and practices. Now, however, some believe that traditional values are being steadily eroded by the increasing pace of change the world over. It may be that if time-honored Chinese ways of being religious are to survive well past the millennium, those vitally interested in that survival will have to develop more formal, deliberate ways of instilling the tradition. Movement in that direction may already have begun with the revival of Daoist seminaries in the People's Republic of China.

Shinto: Japanese tradition generally has held teachers in high regard. But, in the words of one famous Japanese scholar, Shinto is "caught" rather than "taught." As a result, sages, scholars, and teachers do not occupy the place of honor in Shinto tradition to which, for example, Confucianism has elevated them. Human beings are made to worship the divine in all things and to respond in gratitude for countless gifts. Thanksgiving is the wisdom of Shinto. One can encourage it, but most of all it is itself a gift. Shinto tradition emphasizes first-hand experience of the world and of one's place in it. As a result, private schools equivalent to "parochial" educational systems in some other traditions have not been institutionally significant in the history of Shinto.

Perhaps the closest thing to structured education in Shinto beliefs and values has been occasional government attempts to insert components of Shinto—i.e., traditional or national Japanese—ethics into school curricula. In 1937, for example, the Ministry of Education incorporated themes from an 1890 imperial document on education in a new ethics curriculum called "Principles of the National Entity" *(kokutai no hongi)*. Meant to implement the concept of "State Shinto," the document emphasizes the historicity of the classic mythical narratives concerning the emperor's divine descent. It praises unquestioning dedication to the corporate good of the Japanese people under the virtuous rule of the emperor. These pre-war governmental actions, however, are entirely different from the sort of grass-roots instinct that has given rise to private religious schools in traditions such as Islam and Christianity, for example. To that there is really no Shinto parallel. In fact, the Meiji and subsequent regimes' attempts to teach ethics from on high, so to speak, explicitly forbade religious education on the local or shrine level. Since World War II, however, numerous shrines throughout Japan have developed programs for children and young people, including nursery schools and kindergartens. But these are exclusively social and cultural, rather than religiously educational, developments.

83. What other *religious institutions* have supported community life in Chinese and Japanese traditions?

Confucianism: Throughout history, various Confucian societies of lay persons have come and gone. Few of those have been more than local or regional. But since Confucian community is composed exclusively of laity, there have been no Confucian priesthood, no religious orders, and no monastic life. The single most important organizational structure has been that of the Literati class with its elaborate hierarchy and system of advancement determined by examinations. Apart from that, Chinese authorities have often regarded as subversive all attempts to form separate groups within society as a whole. There have been times in Chinese history when prominent Literati have withdrawn from society, opting for the eremitical life. These reclusive types borrowed a page from the Buddhist phenomenon of the solitary monk, but the Confucian hermits were by definition loners and not at all inclined to band together.

Daoism: Monastic institutions have been of great importance in the history of Daoism. Celibate monks adhere to demanding disciplinary codes. The five basic rules of Daoist monastic life are not unlike some of the essential regulations of Buddhist laity. Monks are forbidden to take life, to eat meat or drink alcohol, to lie or steal, or to engage in sexual activity including, of course, marriage. But like their Buddhist counterparts, Daoist monks face far more demands as well. Fasting is a large element in monastic life, including ten fast days each month plus dozens of others scattered throughout the year.

Different orders required adherence to additional regulations varying in number from ten to several dozen. Some orders structured their membership according to levels of spiritual attainment. For example, the Realization of Truth school had three grades among its monks. "Noble transformation" characterized the "Master of Excellent Conduct" who successfully managed the first set of challenges. Abiding by a set of three hundred specific regulations brought a monk to the level of "Master of Noble Virtue." To achieve the level of "Nobility in the Dao," aspirants had to match the Immortals themselves in virtue.

Shinto: An important organization is the shrine guild *(miyaza),* composed of village elders who share responsibility for their local clan or parish shrine. Each man agrees to oversee shrine affairs for a full year. Other organizations called *kosha* have occasionally sought to raise funds to send members on pilgrimage or to galvanize public support for some particular project such as shrine renovation. Some of those groups eventually grew into the various Shinto sects of modern times. Various groups known as *sodaikai, ujikokai,* and *ujikosodai* (more or less synonyms for "associations of parishioners/worshipers") have sprung up all over Japan for the purpose of gathering donations and sponsoring festivals. Unlike some other traditions, Shinto is not famous for developing major internal organizations such as religious or monastic orders. That may have some connection to the fact that the Shinto priesthood itself is historically associated with heredity and clan and has never been an ordained clergy as such. There are, of course, exceptions, such as the monastic order that grew out of a sectarian lineage called Yuiitsu Shinto.

84. What are the most important *gathering places* or communal religious venues?

Confucianism/CIT: Three main kinds of sacred spaces have been at the center of activities. Several kinds of venue called "memorial halls" enshrined the spiritual presence of great Literati, beginning with Confucius himself and his ancestors. These facilities go by the generic name *wen miao,* "temples of literature/culture," while those specifically dedicated to Confucius are often called *Kong (or Kongzi) miao.* Until at least the middle of this century, Confucian temples enjoyed prestigious locations in nearly every Chinese city—as well as in many Korean and some Japanese cities.

In most Confucian temples one of the more important community functions has been to provide a place of study. Confucian temples tend to draw clientele from a wider area than do CCT temples, which function more like local parishes. Unlike Buddhist and CCT temples, Confucian temples do not hum with the ritual devotions of a steady stream of worshipers. There the ritual is more likely to be quiet academic work in the side rooms provided for that purpose. Once dedicated to the reading of the Confucian classics, these rooms now provide students whose homes are crowded and noisy a place where they can concentrate on any academic subject.

Second in importance and number are three different types of altars for the worship of agricultural deities, natural powers of mountain and river, and ancestral spirits. Generally set in a shared compound were the first two kinds of altar, twenty foot square platforms, walled in and facing west. Temples of the imperial cult, finally, could be either of grand scale, as in Beijing's Temple of Heaven, or relatively humble, as in a local temple to the earth deity. All three venues provided a variety of circumstances under which communities have come together.

Daoism/CCT: By far the most important Daoist and CCT gathering places are local temples and shrines, as well as the elaborate but temporary altars set up in open spaces for the larger religious ceremonies. Temples vary in size and wealth and, naturally, the smaller the temple the more likely it is to serve a purely ritual purpose and not to have room for other activities. Community temples at the center of towns and villages often serve as multi-purpose facilities. There might be any number of functions going on at one time—classes for children, play during recess, community meetings—while worshipers go about their devotional activities.

In larger towns and cities, other organizations, such as various Daoist (and Buddhist) associations, apparently fill some of those communal functions as well. Most folks still think of Daoist and CCT temples as primarily ritual facilities that also serve as centers of parish life. Temples typically govern their ordinary affairs through an elected committee entrusted with all major decisions having to do with the ritual calendar, maintenance, and finances.

Perhaps the most important Daoist communal sacred space other than the temple is the spectacular yet temporary structure unobtrusively called an altar *(tan).* Usually set up in large open fields or vacant lots, multi-level facades made of bamboo and covered with colorfully decorated paper simulate grand architectural spaces. These altars are the scene of the major festivals *(jiao)* that extend over several days. They enshrine such popular deities as the Jade Emperor and Zhang Daoling. Afterward, the altars are taken down and the decorations burned. Several other ritual venues have been important as well, though not all were intended for larger gatherings. Organizations within the various sectarian movements that have come and gone throughout the history of Daoism have typically practiced their own unique and often esoteric rituals. Always preceded by elaborate purification, these specialized rituals could take place either in a natural setting, such as remote mountain retreats, or in enclosed meditative venues called "purity chambers." There initiates would closet themselves for lengthy periods of disciplined mental focusing.

Shinto: Larger shrines provide the principal venue for Shinto community gatherings. The more elaborate shrines might have a dozen or more separate structures, each designed for a specific function. The ritual center includes facilities along the entry path for purification by water, as well as the various halls of worship and the sanctuary itself. There is often a separate facility in which the shrine ritual specialists purify themselves. Secondary shrine functions include a wide range of activities. Smaller buildings provide facilities for weddings *(gishikiden),* sacred dance and performance of plays *(kaguraden),* and storage of the portable processional shrines called *mikoshi.* There is also generally a sacred kitchen for preparing offerings and a small shop where worshipers can purchase mementos and items such as cards on which to write petitions to be hung on special boards outside the main worship hall.

Officials administer the whole operation from a shrine office, looking after all the more mundane concerns that are associated with any institution. These include everything from scheduling of events and staff to arranging for supplies and paying bills. Smaller shrines naturally have fewer separate facilities, and the smallest often do not have resident priests. Shrines are organized in a variety of ways. Some are directly under the management of hereditary priestly families still connected with powerful clans of old. Committees of local elders oversee many village shrines that lack permanent priests. Trade guilds called *za* still worship together and manage their own shrines. Wealthy families sometimes even own and administer shrines just for their private use. Finally, some historic Buddhist temples have set up and maintained shrines in hopes of securing the protection of the *kami* for the temple. Some larger shrines attract worshipers from all over Japan, while most local shrines have relatively stable memberships of parishioners. But parishioners often have family or devotional ties to more than one local shrine.

85. Are there standard forms of *group liturgical worship?*

Confucianism/CIT: Confucianism is surely among the most ritual-conscious traditions in history. Each day in the life of a Confucian is full of an awareness of the importance of ritualized actions and ways of thinking. But apart from the larger annual or semi-annual public ceremonies, and the regular acknowledgment of revered ancestors, there is no communal Confucian liturgy as such.

Confucian temples function principally as memorial halls. They are dedicated to the veneration and appreciation of the great sages, teachers, and scholars of the tradition. Honoring the spirit and teaching of the great ones is not quite the same as praying to them the way some people pray to deities or to saints believed to have the power of intercession. Honoring the great Confucian figures generally lacks the kind of spontaneity one finds in the much busier Daoist and CCT temples. Confucian rituals tend to be more reserved and orderly and associated with specific occasions. Popular devotion, on the other hand, occurs virtually around the clock, seven days a week.

Daoism/CCT: Most of the daily ritual activity one can observe at temples consists of individual or family worship. At various times during the day, members of pious organizations may gather for group chanting of liturgical prayers. The priest may address a sermon to such gatherings as well. Major Daoist sects have devised their own communal rituals, some of which have survived intact into our time and are still practiced, especially in rural areas and more traditional villages. Many of these involve group chanting of sacred texts in imitation of the chanting of the assembled gods themselves when they created the universe.

One important communal ritual is that based on the teachings of the Lingbao sect. Elaborately theatrical liturgies address issues and powers in three levels or "registers," the celestial, the terrestrial, and the human. The Golden Register of rituals honors the family of the emperor at the celestial level. A terrestrial level called the Yellow Register is aimed at peaceful rest for the deceased. The now discontinued Jade Register once focused on securing salvation for all people. Officiants and their ritual implements mediate between the divine and human participants. Rites once dedicated to the emperor and his court are now undertaken on behalf of local or family groups of ordinary folk known to uphold religious standards.

Observances begin with an evening or vespers prayer to announce the start of the rituals and symbolically reconstruct a sacred realm in which to enact the rites. Great attention goes into setting the ritual scene, a miniature of the cosmos with gates at the four cardinal directions. Action resumes the next morning with a fast and an offering. Imitating a creative divine act, the officiant recreates the sacred space by pacing out creation and journeys symbolically to the heavens to bring down celestial powers. As part of the ritual the master (or priest) meditates silently, focusing on visual imagery as a way of bringing health to the assembled people. The entire ritual culminates the next day with the master facing the assembly as one now returned to earth. He then dismantles the altar, burns the sacred texts, and sends the deities back to their heavenly abodes.

One of the most important and easily observable temple rituals involves the offering of incense. Worshipers buy three slender sticks of incense at a small temple shop that supplies a variety of materials for different sorts of offerings. Devotees can make their offerings either at the main altar or at any of a number of side or subordinate altars, depending on the size of the temple and on which deity they choose to address. Those who wish to worship at the main shrine may first approach the large incense kettle that normally stands in the central courtyard. Igniting their incense sticks, they hold them upright between folded hands, wave them before the deity, and bow from the waist toward the object of their devotion. After prayer they insert the handles of the burning incense wands into the sand and ashes in the kettle. On some occasions a devotee might have his or her sticks placed in a holder on an altar. Some take incense ash home for use as a curative medicine.

Equally important is a more ritually generic type of devotional prayer in which devotees supplicate the various deities for favors. Worshipers generally kneel to address the chosen deity, praying either aloud or in silence, either bowing humbly or looking at the image. Offerings other than incense include a variety of foods, most commonly fruits, rice, vegetables, wine, and sweets. When worshipers make such offerings, they often have a temple staff member light a candle for them on the altar. Toward the end of a typical episode of temple worship, devotees will burn symbolic

Woman places burning wands of incense into a kettle filled with sand in the courtyard of Long Shan temple in Taipei, Taiwan.

imitation paper money as an offering. All temples provide one or more small furnaces in which worshipers offer gold paper to the deities and silver to ancestors. These burnt offerings symbolize personal sacrifice in hope of blessing and commitment to the ongoing well-being of departed family members.

Shinto: Communal worship is not a daily, or even weekly, feature of Shinto liturgical practice. People may arrive at a shrine in large numbers, but they generally do not gather to worship as a large congregation. Individual and small group worship is the norm, whether for brief impromptu visits made outside the shrine or for more elaborate priestly rituals in the worship hall. A distinctive feature of Shinto architecture is the absence of worship spaces large enough to accommodate sizable congregations. By contrast, for example, the bigger Japanese Buddhist temples provide for large groups in a single worship space. Even in larger Shinto shrines, the parts of the worship facility open to the public are in any case not fully enclosed. Being very much at the mercy of cold weather is the price of wanting a sacred space to be as much in tune with nature as possible. This state of affairs also reflects the underlying sense that people build community through other activities, but perform their most intimate spiritual duties as individuals or families.

86.   What *rites* do Shinto practitioners perform in their *shrines?*

When worshipers go to their local or larger regional shrines, they may engage in several types of ritual called "worship gestures" *(omairi),* depending on the occasion. A simple list of "Four P's" sums up the essential ingredients of Shinto ritual: purification, presentation (of offerings), petition (or prayers for blessing), and participation (of the assembled worshipers). For ordinary, everyday prayers, in which they express a whole range of needs and concerns, worshipers typically make a simple offering before the sacred presence. Alone or in small groups, they enter the shrine precinct and proceed along the path, passing beneath perhaps several *torii* gates, to the purification font. There they take some water to cleanse the mouth and hands as necessary preparation (a ritual action called *misogi*) for approaching the holy place.

Moving to the front of the shrine, worshipers announce their arrival by ringing a bell that hangs over the threshold of many shrines. Ringing the bell may be either for quieting the mind or summoning the *kami.* With or without the bell, all toss a coin in the offering box, bow, and clap their hands twice to summon the deity. After making a brief prayer, they bow twice (one profound and one slight bow) and then depart. For special occasions, individuals or small groups can arrange for the services of the priestly staff. Rites that last from ten to fifteen minutes take place inside the front worship hall *(haiden).*

Various spiritual purposes of the rituals include divine blessing and protection, the opportunity to communicate with the *kami* about countless daily happenings and concerns, and expressions of personal dedication to the divine beings. These services are available most days in shrines with larger staffs, for the tradition has set aside no one day of the week as a canonical day of worship. In larger shrines, the priestly staff also make daily morning and evening offerings to the *kami*. In addition to the various daily rites, shrines host numerous events throughout the year for special communal occasions, as described below *(matsuri)*.

87. What does the Shinto *term "matsuri"* mean and how does it explain the importance of community?

Matsuri is the inclusive word for virtually all Shinto-inspired communal celebrations. The term derives from a root that can mean "to deify or enshrine." These festivities generally celebrate manifestations of the *kami* who have a special relationship to a region or town, though some celebrate *kami* of more universal significance as well. The festivities acknowledge the inseparable link between the *kami,* the land, and the community that lives there. Since it emphasizes the seamless interrelationships among these three elements, Shinto tradition makes no distinction between sacred and profane time. All of creation, time and space, is sacred. *Matsuri* mark those times and places that are more than ordinarily sacred. Just when divine energy appears on the wane, a *matsuri* occurs and renews that spiritual potency. Festivities periodically restore the ancient cosmic order of nature.

Japanese often celebrate *matsuri* with an enormous vigor, an almost uncontrolled energy. Bands of young men undertake strenuous feats of lifting and hauling enormous loads, competing with other groups to deliver their sacred burdens to the shrine or some other ritual destination. That feeling of wild unpredictability offers an important insight into the Shinto sense of the divine as both benevolent and dangerous. Some *matsuri* are explicitly identified as non-religious civic events, but even today the majority are of religious origin and reflect classical Shinto or folk beliefs, or both. Most also retain their ancient associations with seasonal and agricultural concerns. *Matsuri* typically include both processions and activities within a shrine compound. Offerings and prayers, plays, dancing, and other entertainments, and communal meals are features of all the great festivities.

88. How about *worship at home* and through the day, in smaller groupings, when people are not in temples and shrines?

Confucianism: Confucian rituals performed in the home have historically included countless ways of expressing various levels of familial relationship. Of those, the ones that most closely approximate what the majority of people would likely recognize as "religious" are those surrounding ancestor veneration (See Question 91).

Daoism/CCT: Worshipers perform at home many of the same rituals they perform in the temple. Home shrines or family altars are miniature versions of the temple's sacred objects. Smaller images of the various deities enjoy places of honor. Before the image, family members place a few apples or oranges, for example, and small incense pots hold small burning sticks just as the kettle in the temple courtyard does. Many devout Chinese begin their day by offering incense to the terrestrial deity of the home, who is sometimes depicted as five separate figures recalling the five elements. This earth deity is at the bottom of an administrative "flow chart," reporting to the district deity, who in turn reports to the city god, and he to the country god. Offerings to family ancestors and consultation with an almanac as to the spiritual qualities of the particular day are other regular rituals. Many private individuals still practice *taijiquan,* a set of rhythmic movements designed to balance Yin and Yang and maximize energy.

Shinto: Many Japanese households have a corner dedicated to the *kami.* There on a shelf or table stands a miniature shrine building (*kamidana,* which may share a sacred place with the *butsudan* or miniature Buddhist temple) at which worshipers pray daily. For special occasions they will head off to the actual shrine, but everyday reverence to the *kami* happens at home. People can purchase these charming miniature shrines, some done up in exquisitely fine architectural detail, at religious goods stores in any Japanese city or at some of the larger shrines. Worshipers who get them from shrine shops often prefer to purchase them at shrines to which their families have ancestral connections. Priests often visit parishioners to dedicate their new home shrines and sometimes make annual house visits for brief renewal ceremonies. Priests install a talisman from the local shrine on which is written the name of the *kami* to be honored in the home. Worshipers perform a brief purification ritual and then do before the miniature shrine much the same thing they would do at an actual shrine. These rituals, often observed morning and evening, are generally very brief, lasting perhaps three to five minutes. Some families still ritually incorporate in the evening meal food offered to the *kami*.

People with more ample homes and yards might be able to afford larger outdoor miniature shrines called *yashikigami* (*kami* of the home). Miniature shrines range from very simple and affordable to very finely wrought and costly. Business establishments, restaurants, police stations, and bridges on oceangoing ships, for example, might also have a *kamidana* to which the staff make daily offerings. Many miniature shrines have their own tiny *torii* gates and *shimenawa*. In addition, worshipers often bring small votive offerings when they visit local shrines. A popular item is the miniature *torii* gate on which devotees write names and prayers of petition before hanging it on a rack along with hundreds of others like it at the shrine.

89. Could you give examples of some important *"rites of passage"*?

Confucianism: Confucian tradition prescribes a full range of very detailed ritual procedures to be observed for various family, as well as a few public, occasions. They differ from rites of passage in many other traditions in that they generally do not assume an overtly religious form. Confucian teaching places enormous emphasis on ritualized attentiveness to every detail of daily family life. All of that occurs within the larger, presumed context of life under Heaven and in a society that is at least potentially just and harmonious. In pre-modern times, many Chinese practiced rites of initiation for young women and men alike. Families conferred on young men a hat and a name symbolizing maturity. Young women received some new clothes and had their hair done specially. More recently, Chinese social custom has linked these rituals to marriage, now considered the primary sign of adulthood.

Shinto: Not long after a couple have a baby—traditionally about thirty days—they take the child to the shrine for a natal blessing. This is consistent with the belief that all new ventures and beginnings will fare better if brought before the *kami.* In addition, the symbolism includes the belief that the infant thus becomes a child of the family's protector *kami.* Parents arrange with shrine staff for a standard ceremony that takes place inside the *haiden,* or outer worship hall. At larger shrines a senior priest, assistant priest, and *miko* typically perform the ceremony. Pronouncing solemn prayers in an archaic Japanese, the priests then perform blessings over the young family by waving the *haraigushi.* The *miko* may also participate by blessing the worshipers with a green *sakaki* branch. Ancient Shinto tradition retains a class of divine beings called "*kami* of birth or beginnings" *(musubi no kami).* They include *kami* of fire, youth, plenty, and the creator divinities who brought all things to birth.

Several other types of ceremony and celebration are associated with various stages in life. Tradition recommends that parents (formerly the grandmother, since mothers remained impure for a time after childbirth) bring thirty-two-day-old boys or thirty-three-day-old girls to the shrine for a blessing. This "first shrine visit" *(hatsumiyamairi)* functioned as the infant's initiation into the Shinto shrine community. Older children also have their days. Each November 15, a festival called Shichigosan ("Seven-five-three") marks a rite of passage for both boys and girls. Three- and seven-year-old girls and five-year-old boys don their fanciest dress-up outfits for a shrine visit to pray for a safe and happy future. Putting on special clothes is a major ingredient in rites of initiation. Young people reach the age of adulthood at twenty.

On "Coming of Age Day" *(seijin no hi),* January 15 each year, young adults, especially women, visit shrines in formal attire for a blessing. Other coming-of-age observances identify manhood with age seventeen and womanhood with nineteen, acknowledging the difficulty of life's changes with the bestowal of protective talismans. Many older Japanese still observe rites of passage that acknowledge the challenges of aging. They may visit shrines when they reach the ages of 61, 70, 77, 88, and 99 (ages traditionally considered times of heightened receptivity and need), to ask protection and blessings.

90. Are there distinctive rituals or beliefs around *marriage and family* life?

Confucianism: Confucian tradition—Chinese tradition in general, really—teaches that marriage is meant to perpetuate the extended family rather than to create new small social units, all going their separate ways. Marriages arranged by matchmakers have long been the rule, complete with elaborate astrological calculations to assure cosmic compatibility. The equivalent of a dowry from the groom's parents means the bride has been bought from her family of origin. When young Chinese marry in the traditional way, the new couple virtually fuse with the husband's family of origin. As long as an older male survives in the groom's family, the groom and his wife own no property. Most striking of all, perhaps, is that the bride no longer makes ritual offerings to her own family, but only to her husband's ancestors. Young married couples have historically felt enormous pressure to produce a male heir for the family. Traditional Chinese marriage rituals have not generally been considered sacramental as in some other traditions. Nor is marriage a purely civil matter, for the family has been the custodian of the sacred in Chinese tradition.

Shinto: Weddings in Japan have traditionally followed Shinto ritual and the vast majority still include Shinto elements even when performed in connection with other traditions, such as Christianity. Until recent times, however, weddings occurred in homes and were performed by lay persons only. Since the mid-nineteenth century, shrine nuptials performed by Shinto priests have been more common. A ceremony called *shinzen kekkon* (nuptials in the presence of *kami*) may take place in a wedding hall on shrine grounds or in other public spaces. According to some, a marriage deity called Musubi no Kami ("the god who ties the knot") is a Japanese counterpart to the moon-dwelling Daoist Yue Lao who bound together the feet of marriage partners. Many Japanese continue the ancient practice of arranged marriage, and some young couples still live with the groom's family, following Confucian traditions. At the heart of the wedding ceremony is a shared drink of sake (rice wine). Many Japanese families still value elaborate ritual as a form of social communication, and some will even have two ceremonies, one Shinto and one Christian, for example. Daoist-influenced traditions still recommend that couples be wed only on days determined to be auspicious.

Many Japanese active in Shinto communities are also active in Buddhist circles. They do not draw the kinds of clear boundaries between religious traditions that many members of other faiths may be inclined to draw. Traditionally minded Japanese are therefore far less concerned with questions of religious affiliation than with cultural and ethnic identity. Significant numbers of Japanese would like to have their sons and daughters marry in a Shinto ceremony to keep ancient tradition intact. What is more important to many, however, is that their children marry other Japanese.

91. What are the Confucian and Literati views of *ancestor veneration?* What about Daoism/CCT and Shinto?

Confucianism: Confucius did not invent ancestor veneration, but his teaching placed great emphasis on the practice.

Already a millennium old by Confucius's time, ancestor veneration had much to do with the rather utilitarian belief that malcontent spirits of the deceased could cause great trouble. Better to
attend to their needs before they became disgruntled. But Confucius stressed a more positive note of reverence for those who had
gone before and of maintaining connections with one's sacred
past. So much of what we are is our history. In Korea, descendants
of the Yi dynasty still gather annually to perform memorial rites
with full traditional costume and music. This Yi Dynasty Association maintains dynastic memorial tablets in an ancestral shrine in
Seoul called Chongmyo. To each of the eighteen major Yi rulers
enshrined there the worshipers offer three cups of wine and choice
food. Scholars often credit Confucian influence in Japan with the
continued prevalence of ancestor veneration there as well.

Daoism/CCT: Concern over maintaining the integrity of one's
connections with family lineage is one of the hallmarks of Chinese
religious and social life. Members of each family line—male
descendants from a shared ancestor, with wives attached to their
husbands' lines—acknowledge both the continued spiritual presence and the sacredness of their forebears. Their reasons are many:
expression of grief, assistance of the deceased in his or her struggles
beyond the grave, the desire for blessings, feeling a sense of family
cohesiveness, showing continued affection for the dead. Long after
the funeral and an extended period of official mourning, families
pay homage to the dead both at the cemetery and at the ancestral
shrine in the home. There on the altar the family preserves a set of
tablets, each with the name of one deceased relative inscribed on it.
In very wealthy families of times past, the oldest son would dedicate
his life to looking after the proper performance of the rites, forego-
ing virtually all other activities. For most families today, ongoing
activities include chiefly the regular visits to the cemetery, annual
refurbishment of the grave for the feast called "Clear and Bright"
(ching ming), and daily prayers at the home shrine. At home, family
members make the same kinds of symbolic offerings to the ancestors as to the deities enshrined on the domestic altar. Very wealthy

families have often built special ancestral temples as major monuments to the spiritual power of the dead. Few if any of these practices or specific concerns are uniquely Daoist. It is all part of the broadly Chinese religious patrimony, with some elements perhaps more closely linked to CCT than to any specific major tradition.

Shinto: Ancestor veneration as practiced in Japan arises not from the Shinto tradition as such, but from the long-term influence of Confucian values in Japan. As in China, ancestor veneration among the Japanese is virtually presumed as a way of acknowledging the essential unity of the human family.

92. Has the practice of *religious pilgrimage* been an important ingredient in the fostering of religious community in China and Japan?

Confucianism: Confucian teaching generally did not promote the popular practice of pilgrimage, associated as it was with Daoism and Buddhism. A larger concern had to do with the social and political implications of devotional travel. Many Confucians considered pilgrimage a potential threat to the stability of society. Anthropologists talk about the experience of "liminality" as an essential part of pilgrimage: pilgrims step out of their accustomed social roles, leaving behind the rules, duties, and responsibilities of ordinary daily life. They become "liminal" in that they step across a threshold (*limen* in Latin) into another way of being and thinking, if only temporarily. For people who regard their function as maintaining social order, the prospect of throngs of pilgrims heading out across the countryside in hope of miracles or magic naturally poses a threat. Enthusiastic crowds are prey to demagogues and can turn into unruly mobs.

Still, a parallel to devotional pilgrimage developed among Confucians on a smaller scale. Confucius himself became a model of the itinerant scholar, traveling from one province to another in search of disciples and patrons. Later Confucians often followed his example. Eventually the places in which these Confucian exemplars had lived and taught began to attract visitors. Not surprisingly, the tomb of Confucius in Shandung became a goal for Confucian pilgrims. They were generally in search not of miracles, but of inspiration for the struggle to live a good life. In general, it appears that the tradition of family members caring for ancestral graves may have been significant in preventing burial places from turning into pilgrimage goals. Mountains were also important travel goals for China's Literati. There one could contemplate most abundantly nature's sacred beauty. There, too, was the incomparable source of poetic inspiration.

Daoism/CCT: Pilgrimage has long been integral to most of the major Chinese religious traditions. The Chinese term typically translated as "making pilgrimage" *(chaoshan jinxiang)* actually means "paying respects to a mountain by presenting incense." Beginning in at least the fourth century C.E. and growing dramatically from the eighth to twelfth centuries, pilgrimage practices of the various traditions came to be identified with certain specific mountains, with some mountains claimed by more than one tradition. Once identified as a particularly sacred place, a mountain became the site of one or more temples. Eventually Daoists and others alike developed elaborate sacred geographies mapped out with reference to the major sacred peaks or ranges. Pilgrimage to the sacred mountains thus became a symbolic journey through the universe. On some mountains, such as Wu Dang Shan, Daoists have constructed miniature versions of the macrocosm, identifying its subdivisions with such enchanting names as Jade Void, Primordial Harmony, Purple Empyrean, and Perfect Felicity.

Mountains are the dwelling places of the gods and immortals and as such naturally became favorite places of retreat for Daoist scholars and masters. Mountain settings have other, more primal, symbolism for Daoists as well. They embody the perfect harmony of male Yang and female Yin. Deep within mountain caves spiritual seekers could contact the eternal feminine energies. Popular pilgrimage has generally revolved around visits to the mountain temples rather than around extended spiritual retreats. A deity called generically the Old Man of the Mountain, often depicted with his pet tiger, appears in many temples all over Asia, including Buddhist sites, making a symbolic pilgrimage possible even for those who cannot manage the actual journey. Today, various organizations arrange pilgrimage-tours to any of several dozen sacred sites in the People's Republic and in Taiwan.

Shinto: Pilgrimages of various kinds have long been important to Japanese in connection with both Buddhism and Shinto. Sacred natural objects and shrines are of course the most common goals of Shinto pilgrims, but people do not always make neat distinctions between Buddhist and Shinto sacred sites. What is most significant is that the place has been hallowed by some event or person of great influence in Japanese history, or by natural qualities that betoken beauty and perfection. A distinctive aspect of Japanese pilgrimage is the formation of pilgrimage circuits *(junpai)* that encompass multiple stops at sacred groves, mountains, caves, waterfalls, shrines, or temples, in all imaginable combinations. Most common are circuits of either thirty-three or eighty-eight sites set up in relatively recent times by railway and other transportation companies.

In medieval times there was even talk of "thousand-shrine pilgrimages" *(senja mairi),* with multiple visits motivated by desire for greater spiritual merit. Some pilgrims undertake their journeys as acts of asceticism or spiritual discipline, but most seem to regard pilgrimage as an opportunity for reflection and spiritual renewal. A type of pilgrimage to Shinto's most sacred site, the Ise shrine, has come to be known as the "blessing visit" *(okage mairi).* Another popular pilgrimage circuit leaves by rail from Osaka and takes in sites associated with the "seven gods of good luck," including both Shinto shrines and Buddhist temples. Over four hundred traditional pilgrimage routes still attract Japanese Buddhist and Shinto devotees.

NINE:

CHINESE AND JAPANESE TRADITIONS HERE AND NOW

93. How have the major Chinese and Japanese traditions *spread* significantly *beyond their lands of origin?*

Confucianism: Confucian themes pervade the cultures of both Korea and Japan. Temples dedicated to Confucius have never been nearly as numerous in either country as Buddhist temples or Shinto shrines, for example, and today very few active ones remain. But the influence of the Master is still discernible everywhere. Much of that influence is due to a long history of cultural and diplomatic relations between China and Korea. As early as the seventh century, Korean rulers welcomed Confucian thought as a master plan for political administration. Under the Koryo dynasty (918–1392 C.E.), Confucianism took its place alongside of divination and Buddhism as the third in a triad of essential traditional teachings. Korean Confucianism reached its zenith during the long-lived Yi dynasty (1392–1910). In Seoul, a Confucian university called Sungkyunkwan remains an important symbol of the tradition's impact on Korea.

Confucian tradition came to Japan via Korea around 400 C.E., a century and a half before Buddhism. Early Confucian scholars brought Chinese ideas to the Japanese imperial court, diffusing concepts that would go on to become an integral part of Japanese culture. Today the once-elegant Confucian temple in downtown Tokyo has few visitors and is badly in need of repair. But Confucian ideals of family and social relationships are still part of the cultural air the Japanese people breathe.

Daoism: Daoism has exerted some influence at various times all over East and Southeast Asia. Wherever Chinese have traveled, Daoism has gone and left its mark, but it has rarely made its presence felt dramatically outside of China and territories under Chinese control. Daoist teachings have, however, had a significant impact on Chinese Buddhism over the centuries. Buddhism in turn has transported those usually well-hidden contributions on its missionary road throughout Asia. In relatively recent times Daoism, and teachings that claim to be Daoist, has begun to enjoy increasing popularity in Europe and the Americas, but on a much smaller scale than other traditions of Asian origin.

Shinto: Shinto has gone as far as Japanese emigration and military expansion have carried that ancient culture. You'll see the occasional Shinto shrine in various parts of the Pacific basin even now, reminders of a time when Japan projected its imperial presence beyond its shores. Where Japanese communities have taken root and continue to grow, especially around the so-called Pacific Rim during the last fifty years or so, older people especially take comfort in celebrating at the nearest shrine for festivals. But, on the whole, Shinto has remained about as purely Japanese a phenomenon as one can imagine. Even in parts of the United States, for example, where now sizable communities of Japanese descent make their homes, tradition-minded Shinto priests are exceedingly rare. Some suggest that Shinto anywhere but Japan is a contradiction in terms. Shinto remains ideally a tradition inseparable from the very soil of Japan with its sacred streams, groves, and mountains.

94. Where do adherents of the great Chinese and Japanese traditions *live today?* Are any estimates of *numbers* available?

Confucianism: Compared to the hundreds of millions whose cultures and ways of thinking have been profoundly influenced by Confucian teaching, people who identify themselves exclusively as Confucians are relatively few in number. In China, the ancestral home of Confucianism, very few people today think of themselves as Confucians. Many Confucian temples survived the demise of imperial rule, and the founders of the original Chinese Republic in 1912 continued to hold Confucius and the sages in the highest reverence. As a result of the Maoist revolution in 1948, however, hundreds of institutions associated with Confucian tradition were destroyed, damaged severely, or shut down. Since the Cultural Revolution, which ended with Mao's death in 1976, some of those institutions have enjoyed a revival. Countless citizens of the People's Republic of China revere Confucius but are not likely to call themselves Confucians. Something similar is true of Koreans and Japanese, a very small minority of whom will identify Confucian tradition as their principal ethico-religious affiliation.

Daoism/CCT: Daoism has until fairly recently been an almost exclusively Chinese phenomenon. After the Maoist revolution of 1948, practice of Daoism in the People's Republic of China diminished dramatically. Buddhism had the advantage of being an international tradition and thus of at least limited political utility. In addition, Buddhism qualified officially as a "religion" under Mao, while Daoism was defined as mere superstition. Daoist temples and monasteries were shut down or destroyed and thousands of Daoist ritual specialists had to seek other means of livelihood. Things have taken a turn for the better since the 1980s. Monasteries have reopened, and as of 1995 counts, Daoist temples number over six hundred, with about ten times that number of nuns and priests. Some institutions have even managed to revive formal seminary training for ritual specialists. The Celestial Masters school and the monastic order of Chuanzhen (Perfect Realization school) are the liveliest Daoist organizations in the People's Republic now.

Many hundreds of temples are active in Hong Kong and Taiwan, with many more belonging to CCT than to specifically Daoist groups. Elsewhere in Asia, wherever significant populations of Chinese have gathered, such as Malaysia and Singapore, Daoism and CCT are growing but still relatively small. Active Daoists may number several million, while adherents of CCT may number between one hundred and two hundred million. These numbers seem relatively small next to counts of other major traditions, but they leave unaccounted for the many millions of people whose days are full of ancient symbols and small rituals even if they are not formally identified with the institutional trappings of Daoism or CCT.

Shinto: By far the majority of people who identify themselves with Shinto tradition still live in Japan. There are also Shinto shrines in many areas of Asia (and a few elsewhere as well) in which significant Japanese communities have developed. Honolulu's main Shinto shrine, for example, is a highly visible sign of a large and prosperous Japanese community there. Accurate statistics as to membership are hard to come by, largely because an increasing number of Japanese do not identify themselves as religious at all—even if they continue to engage in some traditional Shinto practices. We do, however, have fairly reliable information about numbers of shrines and active priests from which to get some idea of the tradition's vitality today. Some twenty-thousand priests serve between eighty thousand and a hundred thousand shrines.

95. Are there any *historic monuments* linking China's present to its *imperial religion of old (CIT)?*

Three major Beijing sites stand as relics of the CIT: the Temple of Heaven, the Forbidden City, and Tiananmen Square. Nearly a century since the last emperor stepped down from the dragon throne, the CIT is little more than a fading memory. For many Chinese, the CIT remains a historical curiosity. A large tourism industry has grown up around the preservation of major monuments such as the Forbidden City and the Temple of Heaven in Beijing. Chinese tourists flock to these great repositories of their ancient heritage. Maozi Dong and his political heirs considered the remnants of feudal and imperial society as reminders of a thoroughly discredited way of life. They are mere museum pieces to many, and relics of an oppressive past to others, but they remain important evidence in reconstructing the story of Chinese religion.

Beijing's Temple of Heaven *(Tiantan)* is perhaps the best example of a surviving CIT sacred site. The Chinese long ago mastered the art of creating monumental public spaces, as this temple demonstrates admirably. From its southern gate to the northern wall the complex stretches half a mile along its main ceremonial axis. The compound covers an area larger than that of the Forbidden City about two miles to the north, and it is some four times the area of its original northern Yin counterpart, the Temple of Earth. Whereas the temple compounds devoted to the feminine earth and moon are square in plan, those of heaven and sun are round-shouldered at their rear (or northern) perimeters and squared off (like a large U-shape) at the southern ends, where their entry gates are located. Confucian-Literati concepts of hierarchy in authority structures and in family lineage are based on a patriarchal model and are evident in these as well as most other traditional Chinese structures.

As you enter the main southern gate of the Temple of Heaven and walk north, you come first to the Altar of Heaven. It is a square enclosure surrounding a circular terrace of three concentric tiers—round heaven surrounded by square earth, as in the overall plan of the site. The Altar's symbolism includes its use of nine courses of pavement on each of its three levels—nine being the maximum level of Yang energy. The posts in its surrounding railings, numbered in multiples of nine on each level, total three hundred and sixty, recalling the totality of degrees in heaven's circle. The circular Hall of Harvest Prayer at the northern perimeter of the compound also stands within a square enclosure. Symbolizing the firmament, the triple-roofed structure stands on two concentric circles of twelve columns apiece, reminders of the months of the year and the Chinese reckoning of twelve units of time per day. Four larger central columns inside the circle symbolize the seasons. Like the Altar, the Hall sits atop a triple-tiered circular platform. Geometric and numerical symbolism abounds.

A sprawling complex of over half a mile square in the heart of Beijing has been known for centuries as the Forbidden City. Some fourteen hundred royal rooms, all in single-story buildings, cover one hundred eighty acres. Yongle (1403–1424 C.E.), third emperor of the Ming dynasty (1368–1644), founded the Forbidden City as his seat of government when he moved his capital from Nanjing to Beijing. From this heart of imperial Beijing radiates a network of sacred sites toward the four directions. Aligned along the City's main north-south axis are the principal residential and ritual structures, the palaces of the inner court to the north and the halls of public ceremony comprising the outer court farther south. To the east and west the dozens of subordinate residential and administrative buildings spread out. In a massive plaza before the southernmost ritual space, the Hall of Supreme Harmony, an artificial river runs east-west. Five small bridges, symbolizing the five Confucian virtues, span it. In the various halls along the main axis all the great rituals celebrating the empire took place. In overall symbolism, the Forbidden City reproduced on earth the court from which the heavenly emperor, Shangdi, ruled the universe. Beijing was the last of a series of walled royal capitals. Beginning as far back as 1700 B.C.E., cities with names like Anyang, Changan, and Hangzhou all had their sacred centers. That of Beijing saw the abdication of the last emperor in 1912.

In June of 1989, media coverage of the so-called Tiananmen Square massacre brought world prominence to one of China's most important public spaces. The huge plaza stands directly south of the Forbidden City and is named after the City's massive south outer gate, the Gate of Heavenly Peace (*Tian-An-Men,* literally "Heaven Peace Gate"). In a matter of days the space had become a globally recognized symbol for a younger China's struggle for democracy. But Tiananmen Square had been a powerful symbol for the Chinese people for some years before 1989. Early revolutionary publications spoke of the place as "the people's guiding star," the emblem of the new China. Situated just south of the ancient seat of empire, the square was created as a clear revolutionary response to imperial repression. The open "people's" square was an obvious counterpoint to the exclusivity and mystery of the Forbidden City. Its placement to the south of the palace also meant that the square overpowered the palace by virtue of its greater access to Yang energy—a symbolism surely not lost on countless tradition-minded Chinese. Maozi Dong and his communist colleagues preferred to play off their new symbols of power against the old. They could have simply destroyed the trappings of the decadent regime, but they might thereby have risked investing the former symbols with even greater power in the popular imagination. Better to reduce them to the status of mere museums.

In the square now stand Communist Beijing's Great Hall of the People and the Museums of Chinese History and of the Chinese Revolution, contemporary replacements for the old imperial symbolism. Between them and to the south stands the mausoleum of Chairman Mao (d. 1976), but facing north rather than south as the imperial centers had done for over three thousand years. The destination of countless "pilgrims" today, Mao's Memorial Hall functions as a quasi-religious monument even in its rejection of China's imperial religious tradition.

96. If I visited a *Chinese temple today,* what would I see?

Confucian: Major Confucian temples are arranged along the same general lines as traditional Buddhist and many CCT temples, all influenced by the plan of the imperial residence. Simple but elegant formality sets the Confucian temples apart from the others. Most Confucian temples greet the outside world through a main gate on the south side of the surrounding outer walls. Here is what you would see if you were to visit the Confucius temple in Taipei, Taiwan, whose plan is unique by reason of local tradition. Through either the eastern or western portals, you enter a garden with a pond. The high walls recall Confucius's parable about how great teachings are like unscalable ramparts that preserve the building's secrecy, so that one must work to gain entry through the door.

Moving northward from there, you pass through doors on either side of the main gate into a forecourt that offers further opportunity to shift mental gears before approaching the heart of the temple. Local tradition has it that there the main south gate must remain closed to all but those scoring the highest possible mark on imperial examinations. Since no one from the region ever achieved that rank, the south gate remains closed except for special occasions. Walking northward you pass through the Gate of Rites into the main courtyard, surrounded by rooms built into the outer walls. Immediately inside the inner gate you find yourself in one or another of the temple's study rooms.

Looking into the courtyard you would see the main structure, the free-standing central memorial hall on a raised platform. Until the fourteenth century, most if not all Confucian temples would have had a full complement of statues of Confucius and the other major sages. As a result of an imperial decree in 1530 (some date the change to 1382), pictures and statues of the great Teacher and his spiritual comrades were replaced by memorial "spirit-tablets" bearing the names of the sages and scholars. The main hall's *(dazheng)* central altar houses the tablets of Confucius (named "The Most Holy Former Master, the Wise Kong") and his four most important followers, Yenhui, Zusi, Zengzi, and Mengzi. Over the central altar is a panel that reads "Teach without discrimination," in other words, accept all sincere comers as potential students.

Along the right and left walls of the main hall are side altars, each bearing six tablets commemorating the Twelve Sages—eleven students of Confucius and one of the founders of the medieval development called Neo-Confucianism, Zhuxi (1130–1200 C.E.). In the rooms along the right and left sides of the main courtyard you would see several more altars on which are enshrined a hundred and fifty-four more name tablets, forty sages and thirty-seven scholars on the east, thirty-nine sages and thirty-eight scholars on the west. These major historical figures represent the cream of the Literati over many centuries. Finally, behind the main memorial hall, along the north wall of the courtyard, stands a room (the *jung zheng*) enshrining tablets of five generations of Confucius's ancestors.

Daoist/CCT: Larger traditional Chinese temples, of whatever tradition, are generally laid out according to the ground plan of ancient imperial residences. Like the palace, the temple enclosure and its main interior structures generally face south. Approaching the temple, you first see a monumental gateway that offers entry through the temple's surrounding outer wall. Gracefully curved roofs decorated with numerous small multi-colored glass or ceramic figures crown the gate as well as the main interior buildings. In some of the more elaborate temples, the main gateway opens into a covered forecourt, or a vestibule in which the worshiper can begin to experience the change of mind and calming of the spirit necessary for efficacious devotion.

Around the perimeter of the main courtyard you might find small separate halls that function like chapels for devotion to subordinate sacred figures, as well as for special features like bell towers. But the focal point of the temple, whether Daoist or CCT, is typically a free-standing structure in the middle or toward the rear of the main courtyard. A large cauldron or kettle filled with sand, into which devotees insert their offerings of incense sticks, stands ten or fifteen feet away from the main entry to the shrine. At either end of the main building's roofline (and often on the rooflines of other structures in the temple as well) you will probably see a curious hybrid aquatic creature, dragon-headed and fish-tailed, called the *jiwen.* Popular lore says the exuberant creature protects the building from destruction by fire. Pillars or columns decorated with deeply carved stone dragons spiraling from bottom to top often flank the entry to the main shrine. Smaller pillars similarly decorated sometimes protrude from the two ends of the roof peaks and are typically interpreted as supporting the firmament. Chinese temples often created covered worship space in a portico surrounding the main courtyard, and open space in the courtyard itself. The main shrine may be a fairly large structure, but ordinary worshipers usually make their offerings standing in front of the building, while temple staff perform associated ritual actions closer to the altars within the shrine. Smaller neighborhood or

Main memorial hall of Taipei Confucius temple. Note the dragon columns on the porch, dragon design on the front pedestal, the dragons cavorting at the outer ends of the lower roof's corners, and the tiny pagoda on the ridge beam symbolizing the cosmic axis.

family temples naturally lack the grand architectural layout, many tucked away unobtrusively over small business storefronts.

97. If I visited a *Shinto shrine today,* what would I see?

When you walk down almost any street in almost any Japanese city or town, after not many blocks you'll notice a simple, unobtrusive *torii* gate at street side. Turning to look through the gate you may be surprised to see a small grove of trees in the midst of storefronts and houses. You know from the *torii* that a Shinto shrine is nearby, but no structure is immediately evident. If you walk through the gate and perhaps up a small hill, the shrine will come into view amid the trees as you pass through another *torii* gate.

At the end of the path waits a neighborhood shrine, consisting perhaps of only a single wooden structure. Standing several feet off the ground and too small for a person to enter is the residence of one of the local *kami.* On the "front porch" of the shrine, or perhaps alongside the tiny steps that lead up to the porch, you see several small white ceramic foxes, messengers of the deity Inari. Also on the porch just outside the shrine door you see small offerings of various kinds, including a little wooden box for donations. Uncounted thousands of these unassuming shrines are quiet testimony to the presence of the divine powers. Larger shrines are naturally fewer in numbers but still abundant.

Preserving often relatively extensive tracts of forested land in teeming burgs like Osaka and Kyoto, the great shrines are all the more remarkable. Even in the heart of bustling Tokyo, for example, the Hie Shrine still sits atop a surprisingly high and densely wooded knoll. As you pass under one and another monumental *torii* along the pathway to the center of shrines like Tokyo's splendid Meiji Jingu, you find yourself slowing down and marveling at the beauty of ancient trees. The sheer power of place here is almost overwhelming, enveloping you with a profound sense of the sacred. At the center of the site, you see worshipers, perhaps in large numbers depending on the day, approaching the outer building of the sanctuary to pray and make their offerings. If your timing is right, you might witness formal ceremonies of blessing or priestly offering. Shinto shrines do not present the kind of public face that Japan's numerous Buddhist temples show. Shinto's miniature—and not so miniature—holy forests are vivid reminders of the need to acknowledge the sanctity of nature, especially where the hunger for expediency and immediate gratification threaten to banish reflection.

98. Do *millennialism* or *messianism* have a place in the Chinese and Japanese traditions? Does the sect called *Falun Gong* have any such associations?

Confucianism: Confucius was far more concerned about the present and its relation to the past than about possible but distant futures. He was keenly interested in offering people hope through the cultivation of a balanced society. Some have suggested that Confucius was very much a utopian, in that the society he sought to foster was destined to remain an unattainable ideal. In any case, Confucius did not envision any kind of inevitable cataclysm, an end of time at which the world of history would implode in a cosmic conflagration. Confucian thought has been intimately associated with a traditional Chinese reckoning of time that includes cycles of sixty years, but those cycles do not carry apocalyptic implications. There have been millennialist and messianic movements in Chinese history, but none of importance has arisen out of Confucian or Literati circles. However, some scholars detect in Confucian history elements that have a messianic tone. According to that view, Confucius himself may have fulfilled expectations of a messianic ruler nurtured as far back as the legendary Shang dynasty.

Daoism: Several major movements of a millennialist and messianic cast have been associated with Daoism. One occurred during the late second century C.E. under the leadership of the three Zhang brothers who claimed authority in the domains of heaven, earth, and humanity. They espoused a type of Daoism called Huanglao (possibly a combination of the first parts of the names of Huangdi, the Yellow Emperor, and Laozi) and claimed divine origins for their eschatologically charged sacred text, the *Highest Peace Scripture.* The brothers Zhang established a theocracy, complete with elaborate hierarchies. Toward the end of the second century the movement swelled into full-scale rebellion behind a military force called the Yellow Turbans. The rebellion fizzled even though its leaders considered 184 C.E. an ideal time, beginning as it did a fresh sixty-year cycle.

Shortly after that ill-fated rebellion in the east, another Zhang from an unrelated family organized a theocratic state that lasted from 186 to 216 C.E. Zhanglu claimed the authority of his grandfather Zhang Daoling (34–156 C.E.), traditionally cited as the founder of the first Daoist religious movement, the Celestial

Masters school. Both theocracies hoped to reestablish the utopian regimes they believed had existed in the past. After the fourth century, new and more powerful movements emerged, with various leaders claiming to be incarnations of a divinized Laozi (called Li Hung). All taught the expectation of a messiah and a final battle that only the elect would survive to live on in their religious utopia. None had long-term repercussions. Loosely related by symbolism to the Yellow Turban rebellion of 184 was the Taiping (Highest Peace) rebellion of 1850–1864. It was a syncretic movement that borrowed heavily on Christian millennialist imagery.

Shinto: Mainstream Shinto thought has not developed millennialist or messianic themes of any significance. Some recent sectarian movements, however, have centered around such notions. Events surrounding and in the aftermath of World War II not surprisingly raised questions of Japan's historical destiny for many Japanese. So-called "new religions" of Japan, many with roots deep in Shinto tradition, have been fertile soil for messianic expectations. One such organization is Ananaikyo, which teaches open relationships with and among the "five" *(nai)* religious traditions— Christianity, Islam, Buddhism, Daoism, and Confucianism. Various relatively recent Shinto-related cults and sects have centered around charismatic leaders whose teachings focus on preparation for an apocalyptic end of this world. For much of the 1990s, for example, members of a group called Aum Shinri Kyo attempted to implement the doomsday doctrine of their leader, Shoko Asahara. Conspiring to plant biological and chemical agents in Tokyo subways, they planned the final act of human history.

Falun Gong: Falun Gong ("Dharma Wheel Cultivation," also called Falun Dafa, "Dharma Wheel of the Buddha Way") was founded in 1992 in China by Li Hongzhi and received official approval by China's "Research Society of Qigong Science." Its principal symbol is a circle with a clockwise-rotating swastika at its center. Around the central swastika are four *taiji* symbols, at the cardinal directions, alternating with four more swastikas. The iconographic significance of the various rotating symbols is associated with the concept of chakras, or energy centers, within the body. Within each person, therefore, resides a miniature of the whole spinning cosmos. This correspondence between the microcosm of the individual and the macrocosm of the universe is an important link to Daoist thought.

Falun Gong advertises itself as an alternative to traditional religious systems such as Daoism and Buddhism, and to practices such as *qigong* and *taijiquan.* Its spiritual leader, Li Hongzhi, says his purpose is to bring ancient wisdom again within reach of ordinary people who find the traditional systems no longer helpful. Drawing on Daoist imagery, Falun Gong's meditative method, combined with ritual movement, aims at helping practitioners to balance, maximize, and release their energies. Chinese authorities almost certainly had complex motives in attempting to suppress the sect in 1999 and for some time thereafter. One concern may be the ancient connection of religious Daoism with messianic and revolutionary movements.

99. Are there any *holy places* of contemporary significance?

Confucianism: Confucian tradition spotlights a number of places associated with the lives of Confucius and other major sages and scholars. Only a year after Confucius's death the Duke of Lu dedicated a temple to him in Qufu (478 B.C.E.). Within a few years Confucius's tomb and temple in Qufu had become widely known holy places. As early as 195 B.C.E., an imperial sacrifice at Confucius's tomb further broadened Qufu's fame as a sacred site. Confucian tradition did not elevate any one city to prominence as a center of authoritative teaching, except that certain cities were home to the great Confucian universities. The most important cities were always associated with the seat of imperial government, and that changed often through Chinese history, even during the tenure of a single dynasty. Beijing has been perhaps the most important Confucian city. It was the capital uninterruptedly for nearly five hundred years, and

Confucianism was highly favored and influential through virtually that whole period.

Daoism/CCT: Mountains are the most prominent of Daoism's sacred sites, but they were sacred to the Chinese long before the origins of institutional Daoism. Four mountains marked the cardinal directions of ancient Chinese symbolic geography, and a fifth was eventually added at the center, perhaps in connection with the notion of five elements (earth, air, water, fire, and metal). Each mountain has its chief deity who discharges his own distinctive duties. A number of individual mountains in addition to the main five also possess special properties and are connected with particular deities or Daoist sects and schools. Mount Heming (Szechuan province) is famed as the place where Zhang Daoling inaugurated religious Daoism. Daoists share Mount Zhongnan (Shensi province) with Buddhists as a sacred site. The Celestial Masters school established its center on Mount Longhu (Kiangsi province). Hundreds of Daoist and Buddhist temples have stood on dozens of such sacred peaks. Two related features of Daoist sacred geography are the system of ten great and thirty-six lesser Grotto-Heavens and seventy-two Blessed Spots, some of which are located on famed mountains. These sites are so designated because they are foci of sacred energy. Mostly caves, they are likened to heavenly dwellings and are often associated with religious figures believed to have found meditative solitude there.

Shinto: One of the most striking features of Shinto tradition is the intuition of the world's pervasive sacrality. Wherever the *kami* are, there is holiness—and that means just about everywhere people are willing to look carefully. Places where the *kami* dwell are called *otabisho,* "stages on a journey," and are not necessarily identified with shrine buildings. Certain natural settings stand out as particularly potent. Mountains, waterfalls, caves, and trees have attracted Japan's spiritual athletes (ascetics) and pilgrims over the centuries. Mount Fuji remains a revered symbol of natural perfection and beauty, and pilgrims still consider a hike to the volcano's summit spiritually uplifting. On a clear winter's day you can occasionally glimpse Fuji's symmetrical slopes and snowy cap from taller buildings in Tokyo, sixty miles away, and it is easy to see how the mountain has assumed such symbolic importance.

In addition to countless holy places left as close to their natural states as possible, architectural spaces mark many others as sacred. "Founding stories" *(engi)* record how Shinto communities have chosen certain sites. These mythic tales tell how, for example, a deity went looking for a suitable dwelling and decided at last on one perfect spot. Amaterasu is said to have revealed to an imperial princess of old in a dream that she wanted her shrine built at Ise. Even into relatively recent times, Shinto tradition has considered such hierophanies (sacred manifestations) important explanations as to why certain places are high on the ladder of sanctity and power. But Shinto has not been connected with holy cities as such, the way traditions like Hinduism and Islam have, for example. Shinto tradition has not associated the *kami* so much with urban settings as with pristine nature. Some major shrines, like Kyoto's Heian Jingu, have arisen conspicuously in the midst of bustling urban areas, showing a surprisingly public face. But most represent the cultivation of holy serenity in an increasingly disquieted world. Major publications list shrines according to their popularity and reputation for spiritual success stories, rating shrines according to particular categories of greatest interest, such as healing, help on examinations, good starts in new businesses, and fertility.

100. What do the *current practices* of *taijiquan,* divination, *fengshui,* and accupuncture/accupressure have to do with Chinese religious traditions?

Early each morning, nearly everywhere in China, people gather in public places both large and small to practice a slow graceful routine of physical movements called *taijiquan*. People of all ages can engage in this activity. Though it is not strenuous the way higher-speed exercises can be, *taijiquan* nevertheless puts noticeable demands on an astonishingly wide range of muscles all over the body. The idea is not simple physical toning, however, even though that is an obvious positive benefit. Its purpose is to maintain or restore one's overall sense of health and well-being through relaxed concentration. Proper practice relieves blockages of vital energy and returns the whole person to balance and harmony both physically and spiritually.

Taijiquan routines and styles are varied, with three different methods called Chen, Wu, and Yang most common nowadays. Many of the underlying principles in the practice are of Daoist origin and it has been a regular part of the regimen in many Daoist monasteries. But it seems more reasonable on the whole to identify *taijiquan* as a more generically Chinese phenomenon, since for centuries non-Daoists have made use of it with no apparent direct connection with Daoist beliefs. As for its relationship to actual martial arts, *taijiquan* movement is based on the notion that non-aggressiveness, what is called "being weak like water," is ultimately more effective than trying to overwhelm one's opponent with brute force. Hence, for example, the Japanese term *ju-do* derives from a Chinese term *(rou dao)* that means "the way of yielding."

Many people today seek to determine their destinies with divination. Most common of the methods are those that involve the use of bamboo sticks and crescent-shaped blocks. In CCT temples, devotees approach a barrel crammed full of long sticks containing combinations of trigrams called hexagrams, or, alternatively, numbers from one to sixty-four (the total number of combinations of the eight trigrams). Grabbing a handful of sticks, they shake them and then let them fall back into the barrel. Invariably one stick will protrude higher than the rest and it provides the critical symbol for that individual to interpret. When sticks are numbered, devotees request a corresponding slip of paper from the temple staff. On the paper they then read an often enigmatic or poetic interpretation of the corresponding hexagram. Devotees can also drop a pair of crescent shaped blocks with one smooth side symbolizing Yang and one convex side symbolizing Yin. Devotees pose questions as they drop the blocks. One Yang and one Yin side up means "yes," while the other combinations mean "no."

Fengshui, a term meaning "wind and water," is a type of terrestrial divination designed to help practitioners make practical decisions about living arrangements that will be in harmony with natural energies and forces. This symbolic system coordinates critical elements of time and space to allow for maximum harmony in every conceivable human interaction with nature. All natural features, including trees, rivers, mountains, and valleys, for example, have their distinctive influences on the flow of energy. Failure to take account of these forces can make life much more difficult than it need be. In practical terms, *fengshui* assists people most of all in choosing the orientation and design of the "built environment"—in other words, architecture and urban planning.

A complex geomantic compass allows people to arrange the spaces in which they live and work in accordance with the principle of the "Nine Palaces." The compass indicates where Yin and Yang energies flow. A grid of nine squares, each of which contains three numbers from one to nine, can be used in connection with building plans to indicate optimum placement of particular kinds of spaces within a home or office (e.g., storage, study, eating, or sleeping spaces). This ancient environmentalist system has grown from careful observation of the consequences of human interaction with the greater cosmos. Chinese tradition emphasizes the need to conform with nature's "way" rather than attempting to dominate it.

Neither acupuncture nor acupressure is a specifically religious practice. They are associated with healing, but both draw on ancient Chinese principles that have found their way to the center of Daoist teaching. Illness indicates a lack of *qi,* the vital force, which courses through the body along an intricate system of meridians. Blockage of vital energy causes some sort of imbalance of Yin and Yang. Traditional Daoist-influenced maps of the body associate particular nodes with specific symptoms and internal organs. The whole system is based on a carefully observed network of correspondences. Not only is every part of the human body connected to every other part and to the spirit, but the human microcosm parallels in every detail the macrocosm of the universe. Proper placement of acupuncture needles, or appropriate application of pressure, to the malfunctioning energy juncture along any of the meridians seeks to restore the flow and balance, and hence promotes the rise of vital energies that are the essence of health and well-being.

101. Has the *Japanese Emperor* remained religiously important even with the *Japanese loss of World War II?* And were the *kamikaze* pilots associated with Shinto?

In early modern times, especially since the Meiji Restoration of 1868, Japanese governmental policy included the veneration of the Divine Emperor as a central element. Major institutions enshrine twenty of the total number of one hundred and twenty-four emperors, as well as eleven princes, and focus on their worship. Seven of the imperial shrines are dedicated to honoring the spirits of rulers who died unfortunate deaths. Since the end of World War II, the role of Japan's imperial family has undergone dramatic changes from its former centrality to culture and religion. People still revere the emperor and his household as noble persons who continue to represent and uphold ancient Japanese tradition. Many venerable and arcane Shinto rituals still occur exclusively behind the walls of the imperial palace. Apparently fewer and fewer Japanese have much interest in those ceremonies, and the emperor no longer has the national priestly status he once enjoyed. Still, many hope a royal son will continue the imperial line long into the future, and some few even dream nostalgically of an eventual return to the days when the emperor wielded considerable political power. On the whole, though, it is safe to say that most Japanese no longer regard the emperor as divine and do not think of him or his family as significant religious symbols.

After the emperor Meiji restored imperial power when the last of the great shoguns asked to be relieved of the burden of authority, loyalty to the emperor became a central theme. Prior to 1945, the vast majority of Japanese regarded the emperor, Hirohito, as virtually infallible. Dedication to the imperial person and rule was perhaps the most important element in national unity. Admission of defeat in 1945 naturally struck at the heart of what had become such a central cultural institution. Since most people associated the emperor's divine descent with ancient Shinto tradition, the disastrous defeat called into question the viability of Shinto as a way of understanding the world and the place of the Japanese people within it.

On December 15, 1945, the Supreme Commander of Allied Powers, General Douglas MacArthur, issued the Shinto Directive, dramatically altering the shape of Japan's indigenous religious tradition. Acknowledging the tremendous symbolic connection between Shinto and Japanese nationalism, the decree disestablished all shrines and declared them private institutions. Priests were no longer officials of the government. The Directive replaced three earlier national structures (National Association of Shrine Priests, Research Institute for Japanese Classics, and Supporters of the Grand Shrine [of Ise]) with the Association of Shinto Shrines. It attempted to bring as many shrines as possible into a voluntary organization whose purpose was to redefine Shinto as a non-nationalistic religious tradition. Most shrines agreed to join, and most remain under local administration, entirely responsible for their own fundraising and upkeep. Longstanding tradition, however, does not yield so easily to the decrees of conquering foreigners. A number of major shrines, such as Yasukuni in Tokyo and others dedicated to Japan's war dead, still have the power to stir nationalist sentiment. Even now, politicians who want to play that card occasionally make highly publicized visits to Yasukuni.

"Divine Storm Blast" roughly translates the term *kamikaze* that so many World War II films brought into relatively common English usage. Japanese began to use the term during the middle ages in reference to how in 1280 the gods fended off the Mongol invaders led by Kubilai Khan, a descendant of Ghengis Khan. During World War II the Japanese air force resorted to a desperate tactic when the tide began to turn against Japan. Pilots willing to commit suicide for their nation's honor aimed their explosive-laden dive bombers at enemy warships and went down with them. Ever since then, popular usage has referred to any self-immolating tactic or maneuver born of desperation as a "kamikaze mission." Let me make it clear, however, that to identify Shinto narrowly with war or with desperate acts such as those associated with kamikaze pilots is to miss out entirely on an overwhelmingly peaceful and beautiful tradition at whose core is the celebration of life and the sacred riches of creation.

VARIETIES, SCHOOLS, AND SUB-COMMUNITIES

Daoism

Black Hats: non-monastic priests as well as lay ritual specialists responsible for a wide variety of rituals

Celestial Masters school: Tianshi Dao, second century C.E., arose out of the Five Bushels of Rice movement and is one of the oldest religious organizations

Daojia: common term referring to philosophical Daoism

Daojiao: common term referring to religious Daoism

fangshi: ancient term for popular religious specialists called shamans

Fashi: known as the Red Turbans who specialized in occult rituals

Five Bushels of Rice school: early religious Daoism movement of the second century C.E., associated with Zhang Daoling

Great Oneness school: Taiyi, twelfth century, integrated Confucian and Buddhist teachings

Great Purity school: Shangqing, also called Mao Shan, of late fourth century, claiming a thirty-volume revealed scripture

Heavenly Mind school: Tianxin, late tenth century C.E., emphasized importance of exorcism

Huanglao school: an early religious movement from around the third century B.C.E., named after two important sacred figures, Huangdi (the "Yellow Emperor") and Laozi

Lingbao school: based partly on Great Purity scriptures, and roughly contemporary with that school

Neo-Daoism: general name for several movements that developed around the third and fourth centuries C.E.

Perfect Realization order: Chuanzhen, monastic order founded in twelfth century by Wang Zhe, emphasized meditation and asceticism as means to immortality

Pure Conversation school: Qingtan, a Neo-Daoist school that blended elements of Buddhism, Confucianism, and Daoism

Secret Mystical Teaching: Xuanxue, a third–fourth century C.E. Neo-Daoist movement emphasizing (according to some scholars) the quest for physical immortality

Shigong: "lay masters," non-priestly ritual specialists

CONFUCIANISM

Fajia: The Legalist school, fifth–fourth century B.C.E., argued that Confucian thought needed to be bolstered by more specific legal mechanisms, rather than relying on virtuous example to motivate the people

Kongjia: term used to refer specifically to the "teachings of Kong (Confucius)," as distinct from the teachings of earlier scholars called Rujia

Literati: a class of scholar-bureaucrats associated with the promulgation of Confucian values and intimately associated with imperial court affairs. Many people have used the term Mandarin as a synonym for a member of the Literati class

Neo-Confucianism: a general term that includes several schools that developed from the tenth through the fifteenth centuries

School of Mind (Xinxue): a fifteenth-century neo-Confucian school associated with the reformer Wang Yangming, known for its idealist tendencies

School of Principle (Lixue): a Neo-Confucian school, also called Cheng-Zhu after two founders' names, begun during the tenth–eleventh centuries and further developed during the later eleventh and twelfth. Its hallmark was the elaboration of a metaphysical theory in which *li,* formerly understood as a term referring to ritual and propriety in relationships, becomes a cosmic spiritual principle

SHINTO

Minkan Shinko: general term used to refer to a large number of folk beliefs and practices

National Learning: Kokugaku was an early modern (seventeenth–early nineteenth centuries) development that called for a return to ancient Japanese sources, emphasizing a quest for the purest expressions of the Japanese spirit

Sect(arian) Shinto: Kyoha Shinto refers to a variety of sub-communities that arose over many centuries. Traditionally numbered at thirteen, they include the following, all identified as *kyo,* teachings or schools: Misogi, Shinshu, Fuso, Jikko, Ontake, Kurozumi, Kokka, Shinto Shuseiha,Tenri, Shinto Taisei, Izumo Oyashiro, Shinri, and Shinto Tai.

Shugendo: early ascetical "mountain sect," dating from as early as the eighth century

State/Shrine Shinto: *Kokka* Shinto developed out of changes arising out of the Meiji Restoration in 1868. Also known as Shrine Shinto, it came into clearest focus as a distinctive aspect of Shinto after the Shinto Directive of 1945 coined the term State Shinto as a way of describing official Japanese sponsorship of certain shrines associated with the spirits of those who died in war. It is especially distinguished from Sectarian Shinto

GLOSSARY

bagua: the eight trigrams symbolizing various primal elements composed of varying combinations of Yang (unbroken line) and Yin (line broken in the middle)

Dao: the "Way," unnameable source of all things, immutable eternal principle both transcendent and immanent

Daodejing: the *Classic of the Way and Its Power,* principal Daoist sacred text

fengshui: "wind and water," a form of geomantic divination designed to harmonize all conditions of life to the underlying forces of nature

junzi: Superior Person, ethical ideal fostered by Confucian tradition

Kongfuzi: Master Kong, latinized as Confucius

Laozi: Old Master, name of the man traditionally associated with the origins of Daoism

li: propriety as cultivated especially in Confucian tradition through scrupulous attention to detail in all relationships, as embodied in ritual

qi: (pronounced chee), vital energy that flows freest where Yin and Yang are in appropriate balance

ren: true humanity characterized by the virtue of benevolence, as cultivated especially in Confucian tradition

shen: celestial spirits associated with Yang forces, including various deities and ancestors

shu: reciprocity and other-mindedness such as characterize the Superior Person

taiji: the "great ultimate," symbolized by the circle divided by an S-shaped curve, with dark Yin interlocking with light Yang

tian: sky or heaven, an impersonal divine presence through which mortals connect with eternal forces

wu wei: principle of non-active accomplishment by which the Dao operates in all things

xian: Daoist immortals, historical figures who achieved immortality and dwell in the Isles of the Blessed

xiao: filial piety, central Confucian virtue manifest in all proper relationships

Yang: natural principle identified as male, active, dry, warm, bright, associated with mountain peaks

Yin: natural principle identified as female, passive, moist, cool, dark, associated with valleys and streams

zhenren: the Confucian sage, rough parallel to a saint

JAPANESE TERMS

Amaterasu: Shinto goddess of the sun, from whom the Imperial household descended

bushido: "Warrior Way," blending Buddhist discipline, Confucian loyalty, and Shinto purity

dosojin: wayside guardian deities to whom people pray for protection and fertility

jinja: "dwelling of the *kami*" (*kami = jin,* related to Chinese *shen* above), most common name of basic Shinto shrine

kami: "high being," generic name for deity or divine spirit, including some humans who have been thus elevated

kamidana: "deity shelf," where a miniature Shinto shrine is kept in the home, business, or mode of conveyance (such as a ship, for example)

Kami no Michi: "Gods' Way," Japanese reading of the Chinese characters *shen dao* (Shinto)

Kojiki: sacred text, primary repository of Shinto mythic narratives

makoto: Shinto virtue of sincerity and moral purity

matsuri: common name for festival, communal celebration often with ancient Shinto roots

Nihongi or **Nihon Shoki:** ancient sacred text in Chinese, chronicling early Japanese history

Ryobu Shinto: Dual Shinto, so called because of its syncretistic amalgam of Buddhist and Shinto elements

torii: stylized gateway with two uprights and two crossbeams marking entry to Shinto shrine

TIMELINE

B.C.E.

2697–2597	Huangdi, Yellow Emperor, one of the "culture heroes" in Chinese lore, was patron of ancient *fangshi* or shamans (Daoism)
2637	Reckoning of Chinese lunar calendar of twelve months of twenty-nine or thirty days
1994–1525	Xia dynasty institutes the principle of hereditary succession (Confucianism)
1525–1028	Shang dynasty overthrows the last Xia tyrant (Confucianism)
1040–256	Zhou dynasty: Yijing, Classic of Change, manual of divination (Confucianism)
600 B.C.E.–200 C.E.	*Shujing, Classic of History* (Confucianism)
722–481	*Chunqiu, Annals of Spring and Autumn* (Confucianism)
660	Jimmu Tenno, first human emperor (Shinto)
604	Traditional date of Laozi's birth (Daoism)
551–479	Life of Kongzi (Confucianism)
400	Confucius's sayings edited
389–286	Life of Zhuangzi, Daoist philosopher
c. 372–289	Mengzi or Mencius and Xunzi codify the teachings of Confucius into the foundations of a political philosophy
c. 300–250	*Daodejing* composed (Daoism)
221–210	Emperor Qin Shihuangdi tries to suppress Confucian texts, and transforms feudal China into centralized bureaucracy
c. 206 B.C.E.–220 C.E.	Han dynasty; Confucianism official state philosophy
195	Early imperial sacrifice at Confucius's tomb
c. 140–87	Life of Emperor Wudi of Han dynasty, who made Confucian system as his official ideology

C.E.

1	Emperor Ping proclaims Confucius the "Exalted Mt. Ni Duke of the Highest Perfection"
34–156	Zhang Daoling, cited as the founder of the first Daoist religious movement, the Celestial Masters school
c. 100	*Liji, Classic of Rites* (Confucianism)
c. 100–552	Primitive Shinto shrines dedicated to clan deities called *ujigami* appear
c. 150	Religious Daoism emerges
166	Han Chinese Emperor sacrifices to Laozi and Buddha
184	Rebellion of Yellow Turbans behind a military force (Daoism)
220–280	Three Kingdoms period: Wei (220–266); Shu Han (221–263); Wu (222–280)
251–334	Wei Huacun, famous woman Libationer (Daoism)
c. 300	*The True Classic of Expanding Emptiness* compiled (Daoism)
c. 300	Daoist sect, Sacred Jewel, introduces influential rituals
364–370	Shangqing (Great Purity) school emphasizes meditation (Daoism)
c. 400	Confucianism is introduced to Japan from Korea
c. 406–477	Life of Lu Xiujing, compiler of earliest Daoist canon
618–906	Tang dynasty; Daoism enjoys favor in high places
c. 850	*Kujiki, Records of Ancient Happenings* (Shinto)
650–750	Life of Zhang Guolao, patron of (Daoism)

666	Laozi is officially declared a god in the Daoist pantheon
675	Religious Daoism makes significant impact on imperial Chinese court
d.c. 700	He Xian'gu, patron of musicians, is noted for her asceticism and kindness (Daoism)
710–784	First permanent capital established at Nara; introduction of Confucianism, religious Daoism, and Buddhism; Shinto formally organized as all religions interact (Shinto)
712	*Kojiki, Records of Ancient Matters,* a foundational Shinto text
715	Shinto shrine annexes a Buddhist temple to itself
720	*Nihongi* or *Nihon Shoki, Chronicles of Japan,* a foundational Shinto text
737	Shinto shrines number three thousand
739	Monastic Daoism flourishes during the Tang period
748	Celestial Master recognized (Daoism)
750	An image of the Shinto war *kami* Hachiman is transported from the shrine at Usa to Todaiji, in Nara
794–1185	Heian period in Japan, Shinto's fortunes intimately bound up with the developments in Buddhism; foundation of Shingon and Tendai sects of Buddhism
845–903	Life of Sugawara Michizane, poet-calligrapher (Shinto)
901–923	*Engi-shiki* or *Institutes of the Engi Era* promulgated (Shinto)
916–1234	Northern Conquest dynasties; reunification of China; Chan is major form of monastic Buddhism
918–1392	Koryo dynasty in Korea (Confucianism)

c. 960–1279	Song dynasty; Neo-Confucian revival; canon of the Five Classics and Four Books finalized by scholars
c. 1000–1200	Five enormous collections of the Daoist canon appear
c. 1016	Initial printing of Daoist Canon
1033–1107	Cheng Yi, his brother Cheng Hao (1032–1085), and Zhuxi (1130–1200) establish Cheng Zhu school, the School of Principle (Lixue) (Confucianism)
1119–1182	Sun Buer, female ritualist in the Perfect Realization order (Daoism)
1123–1170	Life of Wang Zhe, founder of the Perfect Realization school, or Chuanzhen (Daoism)
1185–1333	Kamakura period in Japan; Buddhist and Shinto theologians devise theories designed to blend the two belief systems, thus inventing Dual Shinto
1260–1368	Daoists suffer serious setbacks under Yuan or Mongol dynasty in China
1281	Emperor Kubilai Khan burns Daoist Canon
1333–1568	Muromachi period in Japan; Shinto grows as popular religion
1368–1644	Ming dynasty; late Medieval Daoism gains strength; Roman Catholic missionaries in China
1392–1910	Yi dynasty; Korean Confucianism reaches its zenith
1403–1424	Life of Yongle, third emperor of Ming dynasty (1368–1644), who moved the capital to Beijing and founded the Forbidden City (Confucianism)
1444	Anthology of canonical collection of Daoist texts is published

1472–1529	Life of Wang Yangming; leads School of Mind *(Xinxue)* (Confucianism)
1516–1555	Life of Yang Jishang, one of the Confucian Literati, who was martyred
1552–1610	Matteo Ricci, Jesuit missionary to China, steeps himself in classical Confucian learning (Christianity)
1594	General Guandi/Wudi is deified by imperial decree (Daoism)
1600–1867	Tokugawa period in Japan; Confucianism gains influence in the Japanese Imperial government
1622–1685	Yamaga Soko, Japanese Confucian scholar and military theorist, originator of the way of the warrior, *bushido* (Shinto)
1644–1912	Qing (Manchu) dynasty in China; religious Daoism struggles to survive
1669–1736	Life of Kada no Azumamaro, considered the founder of the school of National Learning or Kokugaku (Shinto)
1697–1769	Life of Kamo no Mabuchi; applies philological methods to classical Japanese prayer
1730–1801	Life of Motoori Norinaga, regarded Shinto's best scholarly mind
1763–1843	Life of Hirata Atsutane, influential exponent of Kokugaku (Shinto)
1850–64	Taiping Highest Peace rebellion (Daoism)
1852–1932	Life of Liao Ping; considers himself Confucius's prophet
1868	Japanese impose a system of devotion to the emperor, a kind of state creed (Shinto)
1868–71	Japanese persecution of Buddhists by Meiji emperor

1868–1945	Confucians play important role in the Meiji Reform: restoration of the emperor's divine status (Shinto)
1869	Founding of Tokyo's Yasukuni Shrine (Shinto)
1900	Shrine Shinto no longer considered a religion, but a universally binding attitude of reverence for the emperor
1912	Foundation of Chinese Republic; Confucius and sages held in the highest reverence; abdication of the last Chinese emperor
1945	Supreme Commander of Allied Powers, General Douglas MacArthur, issues the Shinto Directive; emperor no longer considered divine
1948	Maoist Revolution; destruction of Confucian institutions; Daoism diminishes
1949	The Republican Nationalist movement established in Taiwan
1966–1976	Chinese Cultural Revolution; disastrous losses for Daoism
1976	Chairman Maozi Dong dies; fortunes of Buddhists and Daoists in China begin to improve
1980s	Daoist monasteries reopen in China
1989	Tiananmen Square massacre: symbol of younger China's struggle for democracy
1989	Emperor Hirohito of Japan dies, ending the Showa era (Shinto)
1992	Li Hongzi founds Falun Gong (Daoism)
1999	Chinese authorities attempt to suppress Falun Gong sect
2001	World population surges past six billion, with India and China comprising over one third of the human race

BIBLIOGRAPHY

CONFUCIANISM AND CHINESE IMPERIAL TRADITION

Beguin, Gilles and Dominique Morel. *The Forbidden City: Center of Imperial China.* New York: Abrams, 1997.

Berthrong, John H. *All under Heaven: Transforming Paradigms in Confucian–Christian Relations.* Albany: State University of New York Press, 1998.

———. *Transformations of the Confucian Way.* Boulder: Westview Press, 1998.

Chan, Wing-Tsit. *A Source Book of Chinese Philosophy.* Princeton, N.J.: Princeton University Press, 1970.

Chen, Li-fu. *The Confucian Way: A New and Systematic Study of "The Four Books."* London: New York: Routledge & Kegan Paul, 1986.

Chien, Edward T. *Chiao Hung and the Restructuring of Neo-Confucianism in the Late Ming.* New York: Columbia University Press, 1986.

Ching, Julia. *Chinese Religions.* London: Macmillan Press Ltd., 1993.

———. *Confucianism and Christianity: A Comparative Study.* Tokyo: Kodansha International, 1977.

De Bary, William Theodore. *The Liberal Tradition in China.* New York: Columbia University Press, 1983.

———. *The Unfolding of Neo-Confucianism.* New York: Columbia University, 1975.

———, and Irene Bloom (eds.). *Principle and Practicality; Essays in Neo-Confucianism and Practical Learning.* New York: Columbia University Press, 1979.

Dobson, W. A. C. H., trans. *Mencius.* Toronto: University of Toronto Press, 1966.

Eber, Irene. *Confucianism, the Dynamics of Tradition.* New York: Macmillan, 1986.

Eno, Robert. *The Confucian Creation of Heaven: Philosophy and the Defense of Ritual Mastery.* Albany: State University of New York Press, 1990.

Ferguson, J. C. *Chinese Mythology of All Races Series, Vol. VIII.* Boston: Marshall Jones, 1928.

Feuchtwang, S. *The Imperial Metaphor.* New York: Routledge, 1992.

Gerth, Hans H. *The Religion of China: Confucianism and Taoism.* New York: Free Press, 1968.

Holdsworth, May. *The Forbidden City*. New York: Oxford University Press, 1998.

Lee, Hwan Chang. *Confucius, Christ and Co-partnership: Competing Liturgies for the Soul of Korean American Women*. Lanham, Md.: University Press of America, 1994.

Legge, James. *The Religions of China. Confucianism and Taoism Described and Compared with Christianity*. London: Hodder and Stoughton, 1880.

Liu, Laurence G. *Chinese Architecture*. New York: Rizzoli, 1989.

Louie, Kam. *Critiques of Confucius in Contemporary China*. New York: St. Martin's Press 1980.

Maccines, Donald E. *Religion in China Today: Policy and Practice*. New York: Orbis Books, 1989.

Medley, Margaret. *Handbook of Chinese Art*. New York: Harper and Row Icon Editions, 1964.

Meyer, Jeffrey F. *The Dragons of Tiananmen: Beijing as a Sacred City*. Columbia, S.C.: University of South Carolina Press, 1991.

Munsterberg, Hugo. *Dictionary of Chinese and Japanese Art*. New York: Harper Art Books, 1981.

Nivison, David S. *The Ways of Confucianism: Investigations in Chinese Philosophy*. Chicago: Open Court, 1996.

Raguin, Yves. *Ways of Contemplation East and West*. Taipei, Taiwan: Ricci Institute for Chinese Studies, 1997.

Sawada, Janine Anderson. *Confucian Values and Popular Zen*. Honolulu: University of Hawaii Press, 1993.

So, Jenny F., ed. *Music in the Age of Confucius*. Seattle: University of Washington Press, 2000.

Taylor, Rodney L. *The Confucian Way of Contemplation*. Columbia, S.C.: University of South Carolina Press, 1988.

Thomson, Laurence. *Chinese Religion: An Introduction*. Fourth Edition. Belmont, Calif.: Wadworth, 1989.

————. *Chinese Religion: Publications in Western Languages*. Ann Arbor: Michigan University Press, 1993.

————. *Chinese Religion in Western Languages*. Tucson, Ariz.: Arizona University Press, 1985.

Tu, Wei-ming. *Confucian Traditions in East Asian Modernity: Moral Education and Economic Culture in Japan and the Four Mini-dragons.* Cambridge, Mass.: Harvard University Press, 1996.

———. *Humanity and Self-Cultivation: Essays in Confucian Thought.* Berkeley, Calif.: Asian Humanities Press, 1979.

Wright, Arthur F., ed. *The Confucian Persuasion.* Stanford, Calif.: Stanford University Press, 1960.

———, and David S. Nivison, eds. *Confucianism in Action.* Stanford, Calif.: Stanford University Press, 1959.

———, and Dennis Twitchett, eds. *Confucian Personalities.* Stanford, Calif.: Stanford University Press, 1962.

Yao, Hsin-chung. *Confucius and Christianity: A Comparative Study of Jen and Agape.* Brighton, U.K: Sussex Academic Press; Portland, Or: International Specialized Book Services, 1997.

Young, John D. *Confucianism and Christianity: A First Encounter.* Hong Kong: Hong Kong University Press, 1983.

Yu, David C. *Guide to Chinese Religion.* Boston, Mass.: G. K. Hall, 1985.

DAOISM AND CHINESE COMMUNITY TRADITIONS

Bock, Felicia G. *Classical Learning and Taoist Practices in Early Japan.* Tempe: Arizona State University, 1985.

Bokenkamp, Stephen R. *Early Daoist Scripture.* Berkeley: University of California Press, 1997.

Boltz, Judith M. *A Survey of Taoist Literature: Tenth to Seventeenth Centuries.* Berkeley: Center for Chinese Studies, 1987.

Bosco, Joseph and Puay-peng Ho. *Temples of the Empress of Heaven.* New York: Oxford University Press, 1999.

Chappell, David W. *Buddhist and Taoist Practice in Medieval Chinese Society.* Honolulu: University of Hawaii Press, 1987.

———. *Buddhist and Taoist Studies.* Honolulu: University of Hawaii Press, 1977.

Cleary, Thomas. *Immortal Sisters: Secret Teachings of Taoist Women.* Berkeley, Calif.: North Atlantic Books, 1996.

———. *Vitality, Energy, Spirit: A Taoist Sourcebook.* Boston: Shambhala, 1991.

Cooper, Jean C. *Yin & Yang: The Taoist Harmony of Opposites.* Wellingborough, Northamptonshire: Aquarian Press, 1981.

————. *Taoism: The Way of the Mystic.* New York: Samuel Weiser, 1972.

Dean, Kenneth. *Lord of the Three in One: The Spread of a Cult in Southeast China.* Princeton, N.J.: Princeton University Press, 1998.

————. *Taoist Ritual and Popular Cults of Southeast China.* Princeton, N.J.: Princeton University Press, 1993.

Eskildsen, Stephen. *Asceticism in Early Taoist Religion* (SUNY Series in Chinese Philosophy and Culture). Albany: SUNY Press, 1998.

Feuchtwang, Stephan. *Popular Religion in China.* London: Curzon, 2001.

Girardot, Norman J. *Myth and Meaning in the Early Taoism.* Berkeley: University of California Press, 1983.

Graham, A. C. *Chuang-tsu: The Inner Chapters.* London: George Allen and Unwin, 1981.

Jordan, David K. *Gods, Ghosts and Ancestors: The Folk Religion of Taiwanese Village.* Berkeley, London: University of California Press, 1972.

Katoppo, Marianne. *Compassionate and Free.* Maryknoll, N.Y.: Orbis Books, 1979.

Kaltenmark, Max. *Lao Tzu and Taoism.* Stanford: Stanford University Press, 1965.

Kohn, Livia, ed. *Daoism Handbook.* Leiden: E. J. Brill, 2000.

————. *Early Chinese mysticism: Philosophy and Soteriology in the Taoist Tradition.* Princeton, N.J.: Princeton University Press, 1992.

————. *God of the Dao: Lord Lao in History and Myth.* Ann Arbor: Center for Chinese Studies, University of Michigan Press, 1998.

————, ed. *The Taoist Experience: An Anthology.* Albany: State University of New York, 1993.

————, ed. *Taoist Meditation and Longevity Technique.* Ann Arbor: University of Michigan, 1989.

————. *Taoist Mystical Philosophy.* Albany: State University of New York, 1991.

Lagerwey, John. *Taoist Ritual in Chinese Society and History.* New York: Macmillan, 1987.

Le Blanc, Charles. *Huai-nan tzu: Philosophical Synthesis in Early Han Thought.* Hong Kong: Hong Kong University Press, 1985.

Little, Steven, ed. *Taoism and the Arts of China.* Berkeley: University of California Press, 2000.

Mair, Victor H., trans. *Tao Te Ching.* New York: Bantam Books, 1990.

———. *Wandering on the Way: Early Taoism Tales and Parables of Chuang Tzu.* New York: Bantam/Wisdom Editions, 1994.

Maspero, Henri. *Taoism and Chinese Religion.* Amherst, Mass.: University of Massachusetts Press, 1981.

Naquin, Susan and Chun-Fang Yu, eds. *Pilgrims and Sacred Sites in China.* Berkeley: University of California Press, 1992.

Palmer, Martin. *The Elements of Taoism.* New York: Barnes and Noble, 1991.

Pas, Julian F. *Historical Dictionary of Taoism.* Lanham and London: The Scarecrow Press, 1998.

Robinet, Isabelle. *Taoism: Growth of a Religion.* Stanford, Calif.: Stanford University Press, 1997.

Saso, Michael R. *Blue Dragon, White Tiger: Taoist Rites of Passage.* Washington, D.C.: Taoist Center, 1990.

———. *The Gold Pavilion: Taoist Ways to Peace, Healing, and Long Life.* Boston: Tuttle, 1995.

———. *Taoism and the Rite of Cosmic Renewal.* Pullman: Washington State University Press, 1989.

Sze, Mai-mai. *The Chinese Way of Painting.* New York: Random House, 1959.

Ter Haar, Barend J. *Ritual and Mythology of the Chinese Triads.* Leiden: E. J. Brill, 2001.

Van Over, Raymond, ed. *Chinese Mystics.* New York: Harper and Row, 1973.

———, ed. *Taoist Tales.* New York: New American Library, 1973.

Welch, Anna Seidel. *Facets of Taoism: Essays in Chinese Religion.* New Haven: Yale University Press, 1979.

Wong, Eva. *Feng-shui: The Ancient Wisdom of Harmonious Living for Modern Times.* Boston: Shambhala, 1996.

———. *Seven Taoist Masters.* Boston: Shambhala, 1990.

———. *The Shambhala Guide to Taoism.* Boston: Shambhala, 1997.

SHINTO

Ashkenazi, Michael. *Matsuri: Festivals of a Japanese Town.* Honolulu: University of Hawaii, 1993.

Blacker, Carmen. *The Catalpa Bow: A Study of Shamanistic Practices in Japan.* London: Mandala, 1985.

Bocking, Brian. *A Popular Dictionary of Shinto.* Chicago: NTC Publishing Group, 1997.

Davis, Winston. *Dojo: Magic and Exorcism in Modern Japan.* Stanford, Calif.: Stanford University Press, 1980.

Gluck, Carol N. *Japan's Modern Myth: Ideology in the Late Meiji Period.* Princeton, N.J.: Princeton University Press, 1985.

Grapard, Alan. *The Protocol of the Gods: A Study of the Kasuga Cult in Japanese History.* Berkeley: University of California University, 1992.

———. "Shinto," in *Kodansha Encyclopedia of Japan, Vol. 8.* Tokyo: Kodansha International, 1983.

Hardacre, Helen. *Kurozumikyo and the New Religions of Japan.* Princeton, N.J.: Princeton University Press, 1986.

———. *Shinto and the State: 1868–1988.* Princeton, N.J.: Princeton University Press, 1989.

Herbert, Jean. *Shinto: At the Fountainhead of Japan.* New York: George Allen and Unwin Ltd., 1967.

Iro, Nobuo. "Shinto Architecture," in *Kodansha Encyclopedia of Japan.* Tokyo: Kodansha International, 1983.

Kageyama, Haruki. *The Arts of Shinto.* New York: Weatherhill, 1973.

Kanda, Christine Guth. *Shinzo: Hachiman Imagery and its Development.* Cambridge, Mass.: Harvard University Press, 1985.

Kuroda Toshio. "Shinto in the History of Japanese Religion," in *The Journal of Japanese Studies* 7:1 (Winter 1981): 1–21.

Nelson, John K. *A Year in the Life of a Shinto Shrine.* Seattle: University of Washington, 1996.

Ono, Sokyo. *Shinto: The Kami Way.* Rutland, Vt.: Charles E. Tuttle, 1998.

Picken, Stuart D. B. *Essentials of Shinto.* Westport, Conn.: Greenwood Press, 1994.

———. "Shinto," in *Oxford Dictionary of Politics.* New York: Oxford University Press, 1993.

———. *Shinto: Japan's Spiritual Roots.* Tokyo: Kodansha International, 1980.

Plutschow, Herbert E. *Matsuri: The Festivals of Japan.* Surrey: Japan Library, 1996.

Reader, Ian. *Religion in Contemporary Japan.* London: Macmillan, 1991.

Ross, Floyd H. *Shinto: The Way of Japan.* Boston: Beacon Press, 1965.

Swade, Arcadio. *Shinto-Bibliography in Western Languages.* Leiden: E. J. Brill, 1986.

Tanabe, George J. *Religions of Japan in Practice.* Princeton, N.J.: Princeton University Press, 1999.

Tsunoda, Ryusaku, et. al. *Sources of the Japanese Tradition.* New York: Columbia University Press, 1958.

Tyler, Royall. *The Miracles of the Kasuga Deity.* New York: Columbia University Press, 1990.

Varley, H. Paul. *A Chronicle of Gods and Sovereigns.* New York: Columbia University Press, 1980.

Yamashita, Hideo. *Competitiveness and the Kami Way.* Brookfield, Vt.: Avebury, 1996.

INDEX